How to Undo life's Airlocks

How to Undo life's Airlocks

David Mugun

Published by

USA
Business Persons Mentor LLC
16192 Coastal Highway,Lewes, Delaware 19958, County of Sussex.

Kenya
Business persons Mentor Ltd
P.O. Box 35 – 00621, Nairobi , Kenya.

First published 2012

ISBN-13: **978-1470150969**
ISBN-10: **1470150964**

TABLE OF CONTENTS

DEDICATION

To my daughter Sandra and my son Glen both of whom, in their unique ways aided in the writing of this book.

ACKNOWLEDGEMENTS

To Almighty God, for the strength, insights and concentration to have this project accomplished.

To every experience and advice that favoured the writing of this book, I owe a lot.

I thank my Dad and my late Mom for the upbringing and exposure that gave me the confidence to write this book. I cannot thank you enough.

I thank, the many friends who inspired me on to writing this book.

Debbie Basden. Thank you for proof reading the entire manuscript.

Richard Gitonga. To you I owe a big thank you for urging me on. I started with newspaper articles at your behest and now a book!

David Mogere. You are the one man who balances straight shooting talk and a likeable delivery of advice to make your point. After going through one of your training sessions, and from various eyeball to eye ball discussions, I drew my courage and positive thinking.

Edmund Mudibo. You are a friend full of positive energy. Your insights made it easier to put together this book.

Collins Sainna. Thank you for encouraging me throughout the writing of this book.

Noah Mwale. I am grateful for your useful insights and contributions.

To everyone who has taught me something positive, given me a chance to work for you or work with you, this book is a reflection of your positive inspiration.

To my Publishers, this would not be possible without your support. I am most grateful.

INTRODUCTION

My Promise to you.

"Show me one man alive today who has no problems, and I will refund you the full amount that you spent to get this book." – David Mugun – Author of "How to Undo life's Airlocks".

Do not be fooled. Everybody living today has problems. Not a single human being is immune to trouble. The difference is in the approach to our challenges.

We all have varying degrees of challenges and our biggest task is to solve or manage them. This book finds its context in the circumstances that we all go through from time to time and especially in the wake of the changes that our ever-dynamic world throws our way.

We are continuously in search of knowledge and skills required to liberate us from the bondage of problems. Every corner of this world has as many people as there are problems.

Success remains an illusion where the lack of problem solving know-how exists. What is true for many people is that trial and error method is often the most readily available switch mode when problems precipitate.

No doubt, there are many different approaches to problem solving. I have come across creative thinking and creative problem solving techniques.

There are many levels of problem solving approaches such as those associated with Einstein and Socrates. Certainly, they are important and helped in bringing forth the many discoveries that we enjoy today.

To Einstein's credit is a quote that is very much applicable to problem solving. He said, **"The significant problems that we face today cannot be solved at the same level of thinking that we were at, when we created them"**.

It was clear to Einstein that one had to take himself to a higher level to solve a problem. Einstein's statement, in a sense, tells us that it is very easy to get oneself entrapped in a problem and, fail to find a solution if we do not change our approach to problem solving.

Whereas, I find all of these methods and approaches useful, I know that most people just want a simple approach to problem solving.

The problem solving approach in itself should not become a predicament but a simplified road to lasting solutions.

Taking the approach to much higher levels, is to me more of a choice than a bridge to everyday problem solving.

What is also very true is the fact that our modern life has kept us very busy getting on with our careers. The daily pressures of our time, do not afford us the luxury of reading long scripts to find solutions to our day-to-day problems.

It is for this reason that I have chosen to put together this book. The approach, pace and logic employed are all meant to enable anyone to not only enjoy it contents, but to also appreciate its practicability. This book has three distinct areas. These are argument, logic and wisdom.

Argument takes you through the first part covering life traps that cause the problems that one finds in life.

The logic bit is in the second part and deals with the formulas that one can apply when solving problems.

The final part of the book takes you through fifty-three secrets to success in life. Welcome.

Proverb - "For every problem there is an opportunity."

1

WHY DO PROBLEMS OCCUR?

To kick us off, here is a little story about human efforts with all the good intentions..., but you are the judge.

In 1979, at an abandoned mine in Pilannesburg, South Africa, the authorities embarked on a good course of reclaiming some of the fully exploited land discarded by mining companies.

Added to this, were the neighbouring farmlands that provided sufficient space for an animal sanctuary. To this end, some 6000 animals from herds of the available species in South Africa were translocated to the new park. Amongst these, were elephant calves that would have otherwise fallen to hunters, had they, been left behind.

Over time, the elephants grew to teenage hood and began to exhibit destructive tendencies, when faced with little or no provocation.

These tendencies resulted in the killing of over 40 white rhinos and the destruction of trees and plants in the park. Attacks on tourists and game park staff occurred a couple of times and was a cause for concern. These were signs only unique to Pilannesburg, a signal that something had gone terribly wrong. The authorities began to pay the price for interfering with nature.

The orphaned jumbos had no parents to pass down to them the relevant manners and practices acquired and accumulated over centuries.

What saved the day, were animal experts who suggested the introduction of mature males and females into the park. Elephants are usually hierarchical, with gender and age being the determining factor.

Surely, the oldies restored sanity and moving on, they proved to be effective custodians and enforcers of law and order.

The translocation zeal dazzled the authorities so much, that they initially had no room for expert advice. The ripple effect of what they started was beyond them.

It is clear to all, that the importance of parenting, mentoring and the opportunity to grow and learn at an acceptable pace, must be encouraged.

Welcome to problems. If not solved, then someone will wrongfully pay the price. Also, bear in mind that the word **Government is not a euphemism for panacea.**

Let us examine some facts about problems.

1. Problems have been around for as long as man has existed and have either taken man from one-step to the next, or left him worse off than he was earlier.

2. Problems occur when situations in life change and create noticeable negative or positive gaps between our normal circumstances and our expectations.

3. Problems can be either negative or positive. When we are not solving failures, we are solving successes. Having very few customers, gives the businessperson a negative problem to solve. Customers coming in faster than they can be adequately attended to, give the businessperson a positive problem to solve.

4. Problem-triggers are both natural and manmade. Man then has to solve the problems

at hand either to get back to the original situation or to better his lot.

5. Our approach must be proactive. Handle a potential situation before it happens. If a problem hit your radar screen before its effects are apparent, then you must solve it before it gets worse.

It is perhaps easier to write a whole book on all the problems that we face, but that is not the purpose of this book. I will not dwell on natural calamities. I will highlight some of the reasons why problems or challenges exist and within the context of life traps, some of which are easy to identify with.

It is important, to note that life abhors a vacuum. In the absence of a fundamental or an ideal situation, something else will take its place.

Therefore, in the absence of a formula to solve problems, anything else will do just as a road to nowhere will lead you somewhere where you did not intend to go. Life traps, together with no formula to depend on, are the breeding ground for problems.

A number of life traps cause or accelerate the problems that we find ourselves facing. We shall spend time understanding them in the following chapter.

Unknown - "Don't ever let your problems become an excuse."

2

MY DEFINITION OF A LIFE TRAP

A life trap, is the experience that one goes through, when there is a gap between the circumstances in life, and the prevailing fundamentals at play around us. It is vivid, when the prevailing fundamentals are at a higher level than your circumstances.

For instance, the effects of not going to school, or not being schooled at all leaving an individual lacking in the exposure, knowledge and skills required to take up a formal career would be profound.

Said differently, *a life trap is the result of the increased difference between the circumstances in one's life, and the prevailing norm or trend, forming part of the prevailing environmental fundamentals.*

For instance, if one is always the fastest of sprinters in neighborhood contests, and then at a bigger race the same neighborhood champion may find himself left behind in the wake of other sprinters.

Being the fastest in a slow herd is deceptive. It can keep you locked up in a life trap for a long time. *How good you are at something, oftentimes is best measured by testing yourself against peers or would-be peers.*

Both definitions, clearly point to one gasping in the wake of fundamentals that outpace the individual. *Life traps are latent in one's mind until the need for change beckons.*

Quoting Alvin Toffler the futurist, "**Change is the process by which the future invades our lives**". This ties in well with the latent nature of life traps in the mind, up until the future usefulness is realized through the need for change.

Traps can be time based, culturally influenced, gender influenced or brought about by upbringing.

In this book, I have no intention to discriminate, isolate or ridicule any race, gender or creed, anyone with special circumstances, career or culture.

Any examples given in this book serve to advance its contents, as a problem-solving book for everyday use.

Life traps have far-reaching consequences in our lives and can be the reason why others succeed in life, and why others fail or remain average.

The good news is that life traps are surmountable and we shall see this later.

Before we discuss different examples of the six life traps in the subsequent six chapters, let us walk down memory lane, through the indulgence of one young woman and four young men. They were once in the same class in high school. Their story nonetheless has lessons for all, regardless of age.

Habakkuk, fondly called Kuk by his former school mates, was the guy that every girl in the class wanted to date. He had all the credentials. He was clever, had the looks and was good at all his chosen sporting events. So distinct, were his abilities, that no boy in the class could openly dare him to a duel, as he always had the majority on his side. In school, what stood out for Kuk was his upbringing.

Kuk was born to a family of modest means, but his nurture was strikingly virtue-strong and with no known vices, everyone trusted him.

He also epitomised the advice given by all parents. Work hard and secure yourself a good future. The girls obviously saw a good future in Kuk.

His desk mate Judy, equally had the "Miss High School" title and was the focal point of the infatuated guys. After high school, Kuk, Judy, James, Jack and Pete went their separate ways; to different colleges, graduated and successfully settled into the corporate world.

Pete, James and Jack became good lawyers. All of them were exceptionally good at something.

Pete, a raconteur of sorts, was socially the king of strategy and seductive semantics. James, was the factual man who laid everything bare and said things as they were, while Jack a verbally venomous bloke, had a talent for spoiling good conversations.

On the other hand, Kuk and Judy were scientists. Kuk became a civil engineer while his erstwhile desk mate became a food scientist.

While on a legal assignment in a far away town, Jack the conversation spoiler, notices Kuk at a social joint. He sees firsthand that Kuk still commands plenty of respect from his peers and the other revellers present.

A quick chat with someone seated close by confirmed his worst fears; that Kuk was heading in the right direction professionally. He was making good money from road projects. Jack looked disturbed. This new realisation rekindled in him the urge to revive an old duel.

Pent up jealousy could not allow Jack to keep holding on anymore. Old school rivalries got the better of him. He walked straight to where Kuk sat, and began to hurl all manner of impolite words at him.
"I know this guy from high school" he said to everyone, knowing all too well that nobody else present knew Kuk from that far back in the day.

"Do you guys want to know who this man really is?" "Yes!" the inebriated and jolly crowd roared back in approval.

"He is scared of women..." He went on puncturing his ego to a point where Kuk stepped out to avoid physical confrontation. Kuk, excused himself and went home early that evening, but not before grudgingly exchanging contacts with Jack.

A few days later, back in town, Jack joined the boys for their usual Friday evening drink. On the agenda was just one item, Kuk! A school reunion, courtesy of Pete's event organising skills was only two weeks away. The much coveted "**Most successful old boy or girl**" toast was at stake, and every one of the lawyers wanted it so badly.

Between the organising committee boys, it was agreed that Kuk would be left out all together in order to first avoid, and if not, then secondly, to contain the re-ignition of powerful affection flames in the event that Judy was allowed to meet him. To this end, an elaborate plan was quickly hatched. All were to stick to a predetermined script guaranteed to nauseate Judy if she were to ask about Kuk.

On the surface, the three boys were on the same side, but individually Jack, James and Pete wanted the bragging rights of going out with Judy.

Pete had a plan to go off script while taking advantage of his gift of the gab.

The much awaited school reunion day finally arrived, and so did Judy and most of the class, save for Kuk who as the boys had established, actually had not kept in touch with Judy ever since high school.

Just as it was in the old days, Joe and his bunch of lifelong friends arrived late. They had stopped over at the shopping mall to pass time. For them, coming early was not macho.

Pete as organiser, kept his distance from Judy and monitored keenly as Jack and James engaged Judy in conversation.

Jack had his go first, and when Kuk's whereabouts came up in the conversation, Jack was quick to say, "If I were you, I would not go there. If he had an iota of concern for us, he would be here. I met him a few weeks back and he wanted nothing to do with any of us."

Jack went on to talk about how he had tried in vain a few years back to encourage Kuk to have a positive outlook in life, but he opted to take the opposite path.

He indicated that Kuk's peers referred to him as "the potential that never was." Jack concluded by indicating that it was painful talking about Kuk and instead, Judy should ask more of Jack. Judy clearly was irritated by both the disturbing information and the fact that Jack was so full of himself. Pete was well aware of this fact and was banking on it.

As the day went on, James, the man who supposedly says it as it is, got talking with Judy. Unlike Jack, he was a lot more dramatic, hoping to capture Judy's interest.
After what seemed a hearty chat, as judged from Pete's position, Jack, asked whether she had met her erstwhile desk mate after high school.

Judy at first looked disturbed by the question, then she confirmed that they had not met at all. Taking the cue from her open discomfort, courtesy of Jack's earlier revelations, he awaited for the opportunity to rub in further disgust at Kuk's mention.

She then posed the same question at James and as if to concur with her pain, he went on "Kuk? Not him! Tell me of someone else. The last time I bumped into him, I felt sorry for him." he quipped.

"As a good judge of character, I saw it all in his demeanour." He went on, "After catching up on life, I finally figured him out." He went on. "In my mind's eye, I saw that he was in pain as he limped." By now, Judy was convinced that Kuk was a gone case.

Then James delivered the knockout blow. "I noticed that he had been beaten senseless by the harsh realities of life. He must be licking his wounds right now."

Then he pensively looked at Judy and said, "If, you sure need some whipping in life too, then look for him. Please find your inspiration from elsewhere, maybe from yours truly." He then excused himself to fill his glass, hoping to return in time for a little toast and that "...happily ever after" magic.

Finally, and as sure as night follows day, Pete got his chance, knowing that both Jack and James had talked enough about Kuk. He starts by thanking her for making it to the reunion and talks about how difficult it has been for him, getting everyone's contacts.

He avoids talking about Kuk for now, and proceeds to charm her by talking about how beautiful she still is. He tells her of his endeavours to get in touch with her, but all in vain. Then a brief period to exchange telephone details ensues as Pete offers Judy a seat.

"You are such a gentleman, and quite unlike your other two lawyer friends!" says Judy. Pete thanks her for the kind remark, but avoids making his two friends the subject of the conversation.

He then gazes as he engages her on what she does and how they can continue meeting. This goes on for quite a while. As if to now make up for going off script, Pete then makes a call and finds out how far the man on the other end of the phone is. Then he says to him, "there is always a next time." Judy is curious to know who else is on the way. Pete reveals that he was tracking how far Kuk was, seeing that everyone else was present. "It's unfortunate, he won't make it."

He then ends the topic on Kuk by adding that he was actually tracking the progress, of his journey to the party, courtesy of a friend who was kind enough to lend Kuk both his phone and car, as he had neither.

"Could be, his obvious embarrassment, has taken the better of him" says Pete.

In a single day, Kuk moved from hero to zero in Judy's mind.

This story brings out what happens in life as we compete for scarce resources. The wicked mind invariably summons the negative energy of jealousy, greed, deceit, conspiracy, intrigues and selfishness to provide life with its dramatic side.

We tend to find many who are ready to use others to achieve their own selfish goals. See if you can find similarities to this story as we move on.

The story above provides us with a sound foundation to understand the next six topics.
There are gaps that we have in life, that moving forward in this book are termed as life traps.

From the story above, we can pick out the following six life traps.

1. *The positive and negative elements of upbringing, exhibited by the main characters in the story. These elements will be covered in the chapter on the Upbringing Trap.*

2. *The Dinosaur Trap that afflicts Kuk because of his failure to keep in touch, with his classmates. He stuck to his old ways and expected his high school legacy to bring all classmates to him. He needed to be the one contacting all.*

3. *The Information Clutter Trap or Misinformation Trap got Judy the wrong way, as she believed the*

negative information about Kuk because it was coming from trusted sources.

4. *The Point-in-time Trap also affected Kuk, as he did not realize that his schoolmates had morphed into predatory creatures' hell bent on sorting him out.*

5. *The Gender Trap that blinded James from realising that communication with a woman that one is after, breaks down the moment you do not fully bring her into the conversation.*

6. *Finally, the Concept-of-time Trap, that caused Joe and his bunch to arrive late for the function.*

Now let us take on the six life traps in detail.

3

UPBRINGING - THE INEVITABLE LIFE TRAP

This trap is inevitable, because someone else raises everyone of us somehow.

Our upbringing has a big influence on the problems and challenges that we face, or will face as we grow, or the lack of them. We are largely the products of the elements of upbringing.

All of us are either raised in a family, or a functional equivalent of one, that inculcates in us value-systems that shape us into who we grow up to be. Human life thrives on a culture.

Culture has a set of practices, beliefs and diet, spiritual matters or the lack of them, an environment and a communication system.

Culture additionally has daily activities, an organisation structure that maintains law and order and a value system that helps a subscriber to rank the importance of what he or she encounters.

While at University, I came across a communication principle that concluded, that *"cognitive processes are culturally determined"* meaning that the way we think and act is heavily, if not wholly influenced by our culture. Therefore, problem solving would follow the cultural approach shutting out all other options available in the world. For instance, in one culture a thief is jailed, yet in another the hand that he stole with is chopped off, and still in another culture he is praised for bringing home food or wealth.

Our cognitive processes derive relevance from our cultural environment so much so that Albert Einstein concurred with this line of thought when he observed that *"Few people, are capable of expressing with equanimity opinions which differ from the prejudices of their social environment. Most people are even incapable of forming such opinions."* Social environment never happens in isolation, many other people who share a similar value system are involved, and this is where culture comes in.

Let me at this point relive a situation that lends credit to the conclusion that *"cognitive processes are culturally determined"*.

At one of the insurance companies that I worked with, ownership, had just changed hands and as is the case at these times, many changes occurred.

The new management decided that most of the products on offer were not appealing to the market, besides not being aligned to what was offered by the parent company elsewhere on the continent. We got into action mode.

First for ease of administration, the country was halved into two zones. East and West and I was tasked with one of the zones, while another colleague took care of the other zone.

A Product Development Committee was constituted and for the next few months, we researched around seeing what the competition had, looked at what was on offer elsewhere, asked our Customers what they wanted; then collated the data and designed a new product.

The new product, unlike the traditional life insurance product, had a mix of investment and life cover components, and the Customer had the flexibility of determining how much of his premium went to life cover and how much went to investment.

Within a month of selling the new product, the sales numbers were very exciting as the Company began to surpass hitherto unimaginable sales "sound barriers". A closer analysis however, revealed a very disturbing trend.

The dominant branches in the eastern zone registered astronomical results on this product, while the dominant branches in the western zone register increased sales, but not at the levels achieved in the east.

Back to the drawing board, the team noted that when the initial research results were deciphered, those from the western zone had a unique message. Whereas most of the communities in the east largely entertained the investment element, those in the west with an affinity for insurance, were more concerned with a special life cover.

They wanted one, cognizant of the extended family structure. They wanted a different type of product, one with an inbuilt mechanism that allowed the transfer of the premium payer responsibility to another family member in the event that the principal policyholder passed on.

Taking cue of the cultural sensitivities, the team developed a funeral product that embraced several aspects of the African culture. For instance, the grandparents, parents, children and kin within the household enjoyed life cover under one policy contract.

Secondly, the policy payer could change with age. This meant that a parent could take up the policy, and then upon retiring from gainful employment he could pass down the responsibility in line with African culture, to the son.

The son then became the new policy payer, whilst the father continued to enjoy insurance cover in his sunset years.

This product got a positive reception in the western zone and sales were up, in fact aiding the company to break another sales "sound barrier". The Head of Sales at the time broke the good news through an email to the principals. It read, "Another record breaking month..."

What we embrace in life, stemming from our cultural perspective, heavily influences our choices in such a way that I agree with the conclusion that **"cognitive processes are culturally determined."**

If you are in a product development role, please add culture to your product development template.

You may have heard of the children raised by wolves.[1] When returned to human upbringing, their intellectual capabilities had been heavily diminished and the young kids found life difficult as the new speed of survival was hard to cope with.

Their first culture as feral children, trapped their lives to experiences of a much lower culture.

---

1. [1] *Children raised by wolves – These cases are referred to as feral children. For quick reference go to the Wolf trust site – wolftrust.org.uk and read about: - feral children, mythology, reality, Kamala and Amala, Djuma the wolf boy, two dog children, skills acquisition, Authentication.*

The ideal human culture required use of intellect, more than the sense of smell and hearing.

The determinism trap is one of the most obvious traps of upbringing.
You often hear someone say, "When I was growing up, I was not exposed to …early enough" or "If I had grown up in this town, I would be better off".

Everyone knows of somebody who has either shared about missed opportunities or complained and blamed someone else for their misfortunes. Worse still, they do little or nothing about it.

These are, in most cases, traps of conscience and are more of excuses than reasons. The famous neurosurgeon Dr. Ben Carson could not have been the best in his field had he allowed determinism to take root because of his earlier life.

Within our cultural framework, many of our interactions influence the views we have of the world, and ourselves, and these can be solutions or problems in the making.

Take the example of a child who on his first day at school interacts with a teacher or co-student who believes that math is a difficult subject. Two things may happen.

One possibility is that the young lad may take this seriously and within himself accept that indeed math is difficult, and hence create a mental block to the subject that will later on produce results that limit the lad's choice of career, and turn him away to none math dependent fields.

The other option is that on his own, or with proper guidance, the young chap may question the reasons why the subject is difficult, and hence find a solution to this subject.

In reality, many of us take the route of the first option that the boy had. We would have had a second chance, had we had a problem solving approach.

Some patterns replicate themselves unconsciously, and even for generations.

There are parts of the world where men, one generation after another, take pride in the size of their potbellies. The protruding tummy in this case, symbolises both health and wealth. Its absence depicts poverty or the consequence of a wife bad with food matters.

One family member after another intends to outdo the other, with a noticeable protuberance like that of Dad or Uncle.

In the modern world, we know that a flat tummy is a sign of possible good health. If anything, a lot of effort goes towards keeping it trim. Should we say that the potbelly example is a tummy trap?

A story is told about a young lady at her kitchen. She always started meal preparation by placing the chopping board over the sink, and then began with the onions, tomatoes and all the other vegetables that needed the use of the board.

This routine went on unconsciously until the day a friend enquired why she did so, yet her kitchen had a purpose built area for cutting vegetables. She could not explain why, but said that she learnt the same from her Mother.
A few days later the young lady, enquired from her Mother.

She likewise, had no answer as she had learned the same from her own Mother too. The young lady waited for the opportune moment that presented itself when both the Mother and Grandmother had paid her a visit.

The Granddaughter curiously asked Grandmother the big question. She simply answered back. "My kitchen never hardly had space to chop the vegetables" and so she did it over the sink.

Some challenging habits find their way through our willing embrace, because of the trust we have in the disseminators.

For this reason, such habits get very deeply implanted into our innocent selves, and we must find formulas to stay away from those that are not useful.
Our upbringing is laden with life traps. In turn, they either then become problems to us, or opportunities to help others out of similar situations.

The simple observation of the friend in the story overleaf, that led to the question "why do you chop your vegetables over the sink?" is a case in point for helping one out of a trap as the lady became conscious and went ahead to challenge her situation.

There are times when upbringing avails an opportunity for children, to either conform or reject what is actually happening to them, depending on what appeals to them.

I have a real-life story to further this line of thought.
A while ago, I published this real life story in my website *www.businesspersons-mentor.com.*as told to me by a friend raised in a family where academic victories were the expected norm.

I repeat it here to help drive home the point on the effects of one-size-fits-all thinking when raising children.

Parental actions can sometimes set off devastating life traps on children. This story will also serve as an introduction to the next life trap "The Dinosaur Trap".

EVERY CHILD COUNTS AND HAS A PURPOSE, HOWEVER MISGUIDED OUR BELIEFS MAY BE.

Have you ever tried within your power and limitations to do everything for a child, and then s/he fails in all these well-intended efforts? Could be that you provided the best education money could buy, but all in vain.

However, have you ever realized that the opposite could be true as well; that the one you thought of as a failure actually has their success game plan already figured out?

A friend blew me away with a family situation that was a turning point in their lives. It would for everyone else too.

My friend is from a typical African family of eleven siblings, raised by parents of modest means.
"Given that resources were scarce, you had to make the best out of the opportunity afforded to you." he said. University was the destination for the eleven siblings because their Father had set this as the key performance indicator (KPI) of any one of them worth calling his child.

As things turned out, the first nine were spot on with their respective KPIs.

The last two of the siblings encountered difficulties that drained away their Father's pride as one of them attempted to pass "O" level exams thrice.

The older of the two, is a girl who requested to travel to Nairobi City to stay with her big Brother.
Big Brother agreed with Dad that the next best thing was for her to work in an office, and the means to the office was through a secretarial college, which he helped her enroll into and paid the fees for little Sister.

To his disappointment, she discontinued after two weeks and no amount of intimidation and prodding yielded much.

After a couple of empty weeks, she brought home an acceptance letter from a College that big Brother scoffed at. In his words, "She had gained admission to the City Council's **"Institute One"**[2], meant to help those of modest means to acquire lifelong blue-collar skills". For sure, this was no means to an office job.

Cookery was her chosen field and it was about the only thing she had a passion for, considering that she was the best cook back at home.

For the following two years she got excellent results in pastry, her chosen area of specialization.

---

2.   [2] *Pseudonym. "Institute One" is a name substituted for the real name of the institute in the story. Permission was not granted by the council, at the time of going to press.*

Big Brother, now with a big smile, secured her an internship at a restaurant where he knew the Chef.

After a month on the job, the Chef rung big Brother to express his amazement at little Sister's pastry making abilities.
 She had now found, and finally proved that there is something for everyone. The story does not end here.

After a while, she asked big Brother to allow her to visit her siblings in the United Kingdom, and after haggling with her, he secured her a ticket.

On arrival in the Queen's country, things were different. She spent a while helping with housework whilst making new friends. After a year's stay, a Kenyan friend took her to a hotel that she knew had a temporary vacancy.

I will not name the hotel, because my story must go on without a lawsuit. On arrival and after introductions, the Chef asked her what she could do, and she indicated her experience.

The Chef allowed her to do the day's pastries, and he liked what he saw and tasted. From then on, the Chef came in late and drunk, because he had someone to do the job.

One morning, the hotel owner walked in and demanded to know who made the pastries. Without wanting to take the blame, the Chef pointed at the little girl.

The owner then called in all of the management and said, "Word has it in town that we have the best pastries" if anything the month's sales figures attested to this. The Chef was not even aware of this. "Young lady, where do you come from?" "Kenya" she replied.

When asked what qualifications she had, she pulled out her "Institute One" certificate and for a moment, a modest Nairobi municipal institute had matched the expectations of a London based top executive.

Fast forward, the hotel owner, took little Sister to Switzerland for the best training in the business, and of cause she excelled.

Fast forward again, she was chosen to bake the cake made in honour of a first world head of state on his visit to the UK. She additionally, also had an invite to Australia to bake the cake for a senior government official's birthday.

She knows what it means to shake hands with the high and mighty.

She is one of the most respected pastry personalities within her circles in the UK, and at the time of writing this book, she was undertaking a degree course, albeit at her own pace.
She is now the girl Daddy asks all, "where is my daughter?" as she is able to regularly send him decent amounts of money.

Fast forward again. There was little Brother in the picture. He complained that because he was better off academically than his Sister, he also needed to go to the UK on a visit.

A qualified carpenter before his voyage, and as life unfolded, he made excellent wooden doors, amongst other things. Today he is the proud owner of a number of houses in Nairobi. It took his Sister's determination to find his own bearing in life.

There is very little to add after such a story. It leaves us with lessons. Nevertheless, this story has relatives and one of them is that of Ben Carson of the "Think Big" best seller. He was always the last in his class, until he learned how to read. He is now one of the world's most celebrated Neurologists.

Some years back, I lived in the same neighbourhood with a respectable Judge of the High Court. I will always be proud of a response he gave to the cheeky neighbourhood shopkeeper.

The kiosk guy asked, "By the way, I see your son driving around when everyone else is at work. What does he do for a living?" With a lot of pride and ease, he answered back "he is a DJ, and very good at it, and is at work when you are asleep." The conversation ended there and then, and at which point the kiosk man quickly introduced a new topic.

Let us take time to identify and aid our Country's future leaders to be the best at what their abilities show. End of story.

Meredith Willson - "Seven gifts my mother gave me":
1. The gift of right: If mamma saw a wrong, she righted it.
2. The gift of friendliness: making people happier than they were before.
3. The gift of rose-colored vision: mamma looked for the flowers, not the weeds.
4. The gift of fun: mamma gave us the best gift a mother can — her time.
5. The gift of understanding: she was always trying to solve people's problems, or at least listen to them.
6. The gift of thoughtfulness: she didn't wait for something special, she just did kind acts any time she saw the need.
7. The gift of respect: when you help to inch your fellow man along on that struggle to dignity, he loves you for it.

Seven gifts? I could list seven hundred gifts my mother gave me. Gifts not boxed and ribboned. Not always noticed or even appreciated at the time, but a part of us. Forever."

4

THE DINOSAUR TRAP (Named after a real or metaphorical animal claimed to have been the biggest ever)

We frequently find ourselves hoping to change the results of things around us, but often end up at the same spot because we always use the same formula or routine. We fear the unknown, and find comfort in the status quo.

If you sleep late because of frequent night outs, that give you little time to have a good breakfast, since you must rush to work. Then it follows, that the rest of your day remains unproductive, and poor results follow on and on for as long as the routine is sustained.

It is said that the only person who always eagerly wants change, is a wet baby. *Resistance grows with age and experience.* The saying "You cannot teach an old dog new tricks", comes in very handy here.

The unfortunate thing is that many people fear changing their way of life, simply because comfort comes from familiar ways of doing things.

If you never leave the seashore, then you will never discover new lands and gain from the opportunities that come with the new discoveries.

Our inertia to adopting new ways of problem solving, is the surest way of getting into more problems.

It is widely said that the dinosaur was the largest land animal that ever lived. By its sheer size, it had everything favouring it. It had first priority on food rights, because no other animal could challenge it.

It had access to the best habitats, and its offspring had the best survival chances relative to all other animals, yet it became extinct.

Science has now revealed that this happened because its body refused to adapt to the changing environment, and the more things that changed around it, the more they seemed to remain the same within it. And finally, the inside could no longer adapt to the new environment. *Traps do not respect size.*

This is what happens to us when we fail to see the problem signs. We continue marking time, even after the marching orders.

We get to form part of the living dead, and get into a state of helplessness, hence far from being problem-solvers.

Are you a victim of the dinosaur trap? If you are in this situation, then it is time you moved away from being a victim of practices and beliefs, to principles that liberate you. It is time to get a liberating formula that becomes your ally in life.

A man whose wife taught children in Australia told me the story example below.

Regardless of the place, the same would happen in Kenya.

On a parents' day at this school, the Parents and Teachers Association planned an exercise for some parents and children.

The participating parents and children, all received an A4 sized piece of paper, with a small box drawn at the centre.

The instructions were simply "draw what you wish."

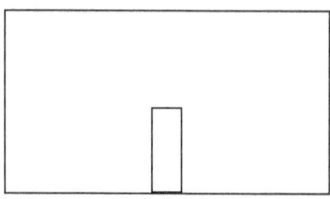

At the end of the allocated time, it was observed that the children had used the small box either as a window, or as a door to a house or car, or as a part of whatever else they drew.

All the parents drew inside of the small box leaving out plenty of usable space. The conclusion was that kids thought outside the box because of their unrestrained exploratory nature, while the adults were all fenced in by previous experiences. They did not wish to take chances. They had been boxed in by the many rules of life so far.

The conclusion was that a balance needed to be struck between when to have a free mind, and when to remain resolute but never on one end throughout. In the same way, dinosaur minded people are never willing to step out of the cage and change.

The children's creativity around the small square, represents willingness to adapt and change to suit the situation.

The parents' self-selected confinement within the small box, represents resistance to change. In addition, as you saw, even if just on paper, it is wasteful.

Anon put it all together by saying,
"No matter how old you are, if you can keep the desire to be creative, you're keeping the child in you alive." *End of story*

The dinosaur trap also afflicts those who choose to stick to practices no longer supported by principles. Whenever there is a mismatch between what we are doing, and why we are doing it, then we are trapped.

To simplify this line of thought, let us read a story told about a monastery deep in Asia.

In the early 1900s, the monks in this monastery held afternoon prayers .Just before the prayers, there was a black cat that was always tied to a nearby pole.

Fifty years down the road, a historian went to the monastery to document the development and history of the monks.

At prayer time, the black cat was tied. The historian asked why the cat was fastened. No one seemed to know, but all agreed that it had to be a black cat.

Helpfully, the historian was then directed to a monk who had retired some forty years earlier.

On being asked about the black cat, the old man wondered how long the cat had lived.

The cat at his time, often interrupted prayers and had to be restricted to a pole.

As time went on, the new monks found the practice and unquestioningly sustained it.

For the respect of God, prayers were to be free of interruptions, hence the tying of the original cat.

With the actual reason lost in the mist of time, the practice of tying the cat became a tradition, and hence the suffering of many black cats.

The same is true of many things that we do today. As we grow up, we tend to pick habits and practices from people we perhaps admire, or do things just for the sake of satisfying our curiosity.

Over time, these practices are deeply embedded in us, and become the default mode that guides all our actions. What is true however, is that our very existence follows a number of principles right from birth to the time the curtains fall. The end.

Now, let us learn what principles and practices are.

Principles are self-evident universal natural laws, timeless, and objective. They are at work whether we understand them or not. For instance, as a man walks by a construction site he witnesses a brick hitting the ground just in front of him.

Had he been one-step faster, the brick would have landed on his head, and perhaps killed him. Gravitational pull was at play, as it triggered the bricks acceleration to the ground.

On the other hand, practices are the exact opposite. They are not natural laws. They are situational, temporary, subjective and depend on the value that we attach to them. Our traditions fit here perfectly.

Our culture means nothing to an outsider, simply because he does not attach value to it. Besides; it is not universal, and hence is only applicable to those who subscribe to it.

Now suppose you had four identical bean seeds. Two of them cooked, and the other two in their natural state. You divide them into two groups of one good and one bad seed. You then send a pair to a friend living in another continent, with instructions to plant and regularly water them. You do the same.

A week later on either end, one seed germinates and grows to a noticeable plant. The other, remains buried in the ground and begins to decompose.

The good seeds have within them the principle of life in latent form. With the right conditions, they make come true the fact that "Principles are self-evident natural laws, and are universal, timeless, and objective; and are at work whether we understand them or not."

The bad seeds, despite the correct steps being applied, made come true the fact that,"practices even if they mimic principles, have no natural laws at play. They will always be situational, temporary, and subjective and depend on the value that we attach to them."

In the second case, the principle of life was already destroyed, and it did not matter thereafter what practices were applied.

The dinosaur mind sees things through unproductive practices, and the more it sticks to these practices, the more the principles that originally supported it are forgotten. Inevitably that mind, in its detached state, now lives in the past.

Unknown - "Most people are more comfortable with old problems, than with new solutions."

5

MIS/INFORMATION TRAP - TOO MUCH, TOO LITTLE OR NONE OF IT. THE TRAP OF CONFUSION.

Are you an avid reader of problem solving and happy living books? Have you read all the books of this type that you can find, and still search for answers?

My personal view is that one or two of them are enough, as this will give you the opportunity to practice and internalize the advice. Too many cooks spoil the broth. Loads of self-development books always end up on the shelf, and the point is missed.
It was self-development and not shelf-development. Diversity of the knowledge in different books, and not same advice in different books, is what is important.

It is natural that learning requires time to first internalise, and then apply what has been acquired.

A friend told me a while back, that education and training is the gathering of knowledge; and that wisdom is the application of the acquired knowledge. Wisdom is best exercised with a clear mind free of clutter.

Therefore, with this explanation too much knowledge with no application is not useful, if anything the clutter caused can keep you confused. Besides, the speed of today's world has no room for one to learn everything.

Do you have friends who seem to know every topic under the sun, and are not experts in what they advice? Remember that these can rub off on you, and leave you wallowing in the miasma of deceit. In this state you are certainly no problem solver, but a problem waiting to be solved.

The effects of little information are also well known. Knowledge and information gaps, always make the difference between success and failure. More often than not, better-informed people have higher chances of success, than the less informed.

Oftentimes it is under accidental circumstances that little knowledge creates positive quantum leaps, as was the case when cement, rubber, paper, the magnet and many other things were discovered. These were all profitable accidents.

Let us not forget the medicine man, who as the story goes, added an ingredient to a rash curing concoction and unintentionally discovered a hair formula for balding heads. The rash infested patient, turned into a zoo like creature when hair grew all over, instead of noticing any improvement to his skin condition. Oh boy!

Those accidents mentioned overleaf, begot big life changing industries. We must however, acknowledge the fact that not all accidents are profitable. Most are loss makers.

Let us now see a local example of this trap in action. Please be patient as I build up this crucial story.

Even in times when information is well intended, the clutter of the misinformation trap will always have victims. These people are perpetually dependent on others for information. They simply are followers.

What does not help things, is the very complex nature of communication itself.

Among the principles of communication, are two that state that –

1. *"Communication is a process." and*
2. *That "meaning cannot be fully transferred".*

As a build up to my example, I will briefly expound on both principles.

First, communication is a process that requires one person passing information to another. The process has a message sent to an intended human target through a medium such as; the radio, telephone, printed means or the air in the case of a face-to-face conversation.

The recipient, then understands the message and demonstrates so by providing feedback by either talking, writing, gesturing or by any other form, depending on the appropriateness of what is desirable.

There are obviously many other mediums available for communication.

Please note, that when information reaches an unintended target, it is termed as "noise", and this "**noise**" will form a big part of my example.

Secondly, meaning can never be fully transferred, and hence the reason why communication experts do their best to ensure that as much of the intended meaning is transferred to the intended audience as possible.

Now suppose I got ten people into one room, asked them to draw a four-legged animal with fur, whiskers, claws and added that this creature is common in our country.

I may have meant a domestic cat but my ten artists will draw a dog, maybe a lion or even a T9.[3]

Different pictures formed in all the ten minds.

Meaning was not fully transferred firstly because of how much I communicated out, and secondly, because of the individual experiences of my ten artists.
These two factors aided in shaping the picture in their respective minds.

With the explanations now out of the way, let us zero in on the radio and use it to help us better, understand the trap of mis/information.

We know that the radio in this Country is such a powerful medium of communication, so much so that anything said on radio is gospel truth to the common person.

This is the reason that the unsuccessful mutinous soldiers of the infamous 1982 coup d'état, commandeered the radio station, that coincidentally was the only one available then to announce the supposed change of guard.

Similarly, on many occasions before and after then, people in high positions either abused or used state radio to advance selfish objectives, simply because on the ground someone would surely say, "I heard it on the radio."

3.   [3] *A T9, is a dog like and usually rabid animal that originally crossed over from a Tanzanian national park into Kenya. They are rarely seen these days.*

Because of its ubiquity and flexibility to reach intended target markets, its availability to send preferred vernacular messages makes for an effective communication tool. Vernacular, obviously aids in the better transfer of meaning.

Hold your patience to my build up, as it is critical to walk you through all that is mentioned so far. Let us move on.

The mass market (majority of the radio audience) on average falls under the category best for targeting simple products, such as fast moving consumer goods like toilet soap because they are simple to understand, besides being widely used.

The more complex products, such as financial products, are best positioned directly to the intended target market unless designed for the masses. Even when intended for the mass market, plenty of information must be provided. We have a problem when complex information is passed down to a market that needs plenty of guidance.

You can now see where I am headed. Remember the "noise" I talked about earlier as you read on.

The Nairobi Stock Exchange has enjoyed unrivalled growth in the East and Central Africa region. Significant changes towards modernisation have seen the bourse compared favourably with peers around the world.

Growth for the Stock Exchange comes through the buying and selling of shares, and any related activities.

Let me absolve the Stock Exchange of any blame, or misconceptions, that my efforts to advance instances of the misinformation and information clutter trap may bring forth.
Financial products, as we have seen, fall under the complex products category.

On the other hand the majority of the fast moving consumer goods, fall under the simple products category. Discussing and grasping the attributes of toilet soap is a lot easier than discussing corporate finance matters.

Spirited attempts to emulate successful people ought to be executed with caution and plenty of advice. When simple minds rise up to grasp opportunities better understood by complex minds, extra care must be taken.

This is where the "noise" fits in. Remember we said that when information reaches an unintended target, it is "noise". Many people think they are prepared enough to understand complex things without guidance. To them, **seeing is believing!**

Many Kenyans admire our national heroes who pioneered in the trading of shares at the Stock Exchange.(Most are known, but their names are withheld).

They grew in stature to become prominent figures; a lot about them is in the public domain and it is known that they acquired part of their wealth by trading at the Stock Exchange. Taking cue from the pioneers, obviously by associating their tangible wealth to stock fortunes, Kenyans got inspired to take up the shares on offer.

Fast forward. Many companies have gone public and afforded Kenyans an opportunity to realize their dreams to own companies.

We have witnessed endless queues when Initial Public Offers (IPOs) are nearing their end. Last minute reactors to opportunities are normally of the herd mentality type. Every single person dives in with his or her intentions. Long term, short term, speculative purchases and so on.

Over time, I have noticed that most of these shares usually drop in value to the detriment of the speculator. **Many people afford to purchase shares on the back of bank loans, and then expect that astronomical growth in share value will in turn enable them to repay the loans with ease, but how wrong can one be?**

The shares normally need a longer-term view, and not the immediate benefit derived from the soap you purchased two minutes ago.

Those servicing loans taken to purchase stocks that are now below market value, have come to realize that serious stock traders are actually not simple minds, admiring them notwithstanding.

"The radio said that we should hurry to take up shares in the IPO," screamed one woman. "I sold three of my best cows to buy shares, and now I realize that I could be making more from milk," said another.
"Noise" picked up by those with little knowledge and a herd mentality, aided these accidents.

I suspect that we shall be seeing more institutional buyers moving forward, and less of the individuals, and especially shareholders of the mass-market mentality who are often seen sound asleep at Annual General Meetings.
Management presents the financials to a few alert stakeholders.

Then later, the sleepy group is seen fully awakened by a pleasant aroma that leads them to a serving point, where they demand for food, as this is the bit that they understand.

When complex products are presented in ways that the simple mind appreciates, the results are obvious. The simple mind bites the bait that may take it to dry and empty land. All too often people miss the principle, and only find themselves executing the practice driven by a supposed principle. End of story

"The man who will use his skill and constructive imagination to see how much he can give for a dollar, instead of how little he can give for a dollar, is bound to succeed."--Henry Ford

6

POINT- IN- TIME TRAP

It is possible to stay frozen in time and assume that things will just move on day-in and day-out. This line of thought is very much challenged by the stage of life that we are experiencing.

To bring us up to speed on this, let us look at the four different stages of man's development. Man was once primitive in his mode of operation, relative to what he has achieved today.

Early man and Modern man are miles apart mentally even though they remain the same genetically.

I wonder how Early man if given a chance, would react to the modern day marvels.

POINT-IN-TIME. STAGE ONE

In earlier times, man was a hunter and gatherer. His tools of survival were the sharp objects that he used either to harvest from the abundant providence of the wild bushes, or to kill animals for a good meal.

The challenges of this time were very much based on finding longevity of perishables so that the hunting and gathering activities would be lessened, but to no avail as this solution belonged to a more sophisticated lifestyle way into the future. Day was day, and night was meant to pass with little or no economic activity, so that morning would come again.

At these early stages, 24 was not even the title of a movie or television series, let alone the 24-hour economy concept.

For man to move to modern day life, there were still a few stages that he had to pass through. The interfacing periods were marked by significant differences, when compared with the previous points in time.

I call the experiences through these stages, the "connective tension," or growing pains.

This tension is coming from the inevitable higher levels of thinking, which had no relationship with earlier intellect.

Every stage is part of a metamorphosis, and when analysed is a total contrast to the normal human body growth phases of predictably becoming a bigger version of your younger self. Let us use the butterfly to illustrate the point.

Literally speaking, the metamorphosis of the butterfly has very distinct stages, with every one stage having very different characteristics from the other. At birth, the egg is just an egg. Round and encased in a shell.

Then it breaks out and becomes a larva, marking this stage by eating its very nutritious shell. The larva is what we all call the caterpillar. In most cases, it is best to avoid contact, as it causes skin irritation from its stinging hairs. The egg and the caterpillar have no resemblance at all, and it is hard to relate the two stages to each other.

Neither is there a resemblance to the next stage, whose manifestation we refer to as pupa. The developing insect occupies one spot, with no noticeable movement for a while. Change is occurring on the inside, while the outside conceals it until it is necessary to show the world.

Finally, it assumes yet another shape unrelated to all earlier transmutations, and becomes a flowery butterfly.

It breaks out of the pupa cocoon, pumps fluids from its abdomen to the veins in its folded wings to straighten them, and gets to fly away.

The butterfly must change for it to get to the next stage. If it does not change, then it will die. Today, we have the living dead amongst us, who have refused to move on to the next stage. Such refusal to change is the cause of much grief, as we shall see shortly.

The metamorphosis analogy, shows us that every stage of human development has its own problems and challenges to solve, and within the form and thinking adapted by that particular stage. In a sense, every stage had its own cognitive process (way of thinking), encased within that particular point in time.

The thinking at each of the progressive stages can hardly provide solutions to any other higher stage, save for comical relief and hard lessons for anyone whose digression in search of a blast from the past, proves regressive. To be safe, let me acknowledge an exception. Some earlier thinking keeps us alive today, if knowledge from fields such as medicine passed down generations is anything to go by.

I believe, that the very early parts of this Stone-Age phase had plenty of presiding males in charge of the tribe, in much the same way the presiding male monkey in the park has the mating rights.

Then the polygamous stage came in. Today the one with more knowledge, or money, gets the bride and has moved from mating to making love.

We still find people stuck in time with the hangover of yester stages of man's development. These men still think they have the mating rights but they are wrong, and we now call them rapists or adulterous people.

Being caught up by stage-in-time traps is a real problem to worry about. The formulas that will be discussed in the topics ahead will clearly show you that the steps are just as applicable to the individual, as they are to the steps collectively taken to solve a community problem or challenge.

STAGE TWO

A few men, then thought at a higher level riding on the back of increased experience, and moved into the agricultural age where crops were planted based on seasons, and animals were domesticated and reared for food, security and wealth.

The second stage was unlike in the first stage, where the macho man was King by virtue of physical strength and skill for hunting and gathering.

The second stage was one of wit and a sense of wealth creation by land size; what it produced and how many animals it could comfortably hold.

There were early adapters, and those that made their way to this age rather grudgingly. It was possible to find the macho man of the hunter-gatherer stage mentality working for a less muscular large-scale farmer, because the game had changed and the ground had shifted.

The smart macho men began to provide entertainment through sports such as wrestling, boxing e.t.c. (not all sports people are of this mentality. Most of them are extremely intelligent and successful.) This stage of course did not happen overnight. Those who were still of a hunter-gatherer mentality, were seen as thieves whenever they went to hunt on a farm.

What may have been good in stage one, was not necessarily welcome in stage two. As we shall see later, all elements from stage one to four still exist in some way, and we still find ourselves entrapped in challenges that can be overcome.

You are now beginning to see that when you are left behind in the wake of a new age, the practices of yester stages assume society-threatening dimensions.

STAGE THREE

The third stage of human development, is the one that most people alive today have experienced, and so did our Great Grandparents. The agricultural stage gave way to the industrial age.

This is where Henry Ford, and the inventors of most of the things that influence life to this day, thrived in. Industries are still very much part of our lives, and many people continue to eke out a living by working in some factory.

Human progress during this stage put man on the moon, albeit with information age technology that enabled man to travel by air, allowed for mass production of medicine and the list goes on. In the industrial age, money was singularly the biggest source of power.

To reach your markets, one only needed to afford the use of television, radio and newspapers. The diminishing sales of newspapers the world over, is a signal that another age has come into play.

Power is shifting to something else. We shall in a little while discuss this metamorphosis, but now let us continue with the industrial age.

This stage of human development has widened the gap between human beings and led to a world classified as first world, second, third and the "fourth world". (Developed, Developing, Emerging and Dormant)

There are countries which have remained exporters of raw materials to more industrialized countries. No value addition comes in to play, and entire populations are entrapped in the agrarian age.

The irony of this age is that the countries trying to move into the first world, find themselves competing with well-established organizations employing the best technology.

By the time your new plant is ready, another one elsewhere is using technology that is more appropriate. This leaves the competitor to play second fiddle for long, given that capital expenses associated with construction have to go over a long period before a return on investment is realized.

It is just not useful to get into industries that are already extremely established. In any case, every region of the world has natural advantages to be a leader in sectors where real economies of scale exist. Just like the other two stages of development, the industrial age has had its victims.

Those that did not acquire the relevant skills and knowledge necessary for the industrial age, found their place at the gates and in the plants doing menial jobs. And at best, talking about how much respect they would command back at the farms, given their physical strength.

What was macho in stage one is now a bad thing to depend upon! Industrialization transformed the otherwise slow rural life, into urban life where industries were concentrated. This allowed all the stages of human development to interact within close proximity.

In large towns, you still find those who survive on brawn as opposed to brain, those that live in nearby farms and supply the town residents with food, the industrialists and professionals with fine habits termed as etiquette, and just about every element of every stage of development.

This age came up with terminologies such as retirement, right sizing, corporate strategy.... the works.

With every improvement in technology, the slow adapters suffered. Imagine what happened to the Secretary who refused to type because a typing pool existed. What if she also never improved her qualifications?

When the computer came in, Secretaries began to disappear as the new term multi-skilled knowledge workers came into being. Again, the traps of yester years are at play in the industrial age.

STAGE FOUR

The final stage that we are now in, is the information age. The internet is here with us. This is where the power is shifting.

Relevant and engaging information is the power. Word of mouth now has a brother named word of mouse. If you can maintain high traffic into your website, then you have the power.

The computer is obviously one of the inventions that has shaped our lives in a way and scale never ever imagined by its inventors. As mentioned earlier, a new age does not all happen in a flash!

You know it when you begin to see the signs. Globally newspaper sales are going down by the day, the internet is taking over. If you are working for a newspaper, think carefully.

The green revolution that is driving environmental conservation efforts is getting louder, because trees used in the manufacture of paper must be saved.

The alternative technology, that can substitute the newspaper is out of reach for many, but only for a while.

If you do not have a game plan, you are headed into an obvious time trap. Likewise, if you are investing in a printing press in this age, you had better have something up your sleeve.

Many people are creating their own communities of markets online, and have a following at a fraction of what it would have cost had the conventional channels been used.

Unlike the radio story earlier on where there was "noise", it is possible to be spot on when targeting a group with a desired profile. It is easier to attract financially perceptive people to purchase shares through a web site that has their interests in mind, and not through a radio commercial that comes in the middle of a program that the financially savvy never listen to.

The information age has its first victims trapped in yester years through what is widely referred to as the digital divide. Those who have access and knowledge of using computers, stand a better chance of thriving in the information age.

Just look ten years back, there are many companies that were household names and have almost completely disappeared. These companies have remained trapped in the industrial age mentality.

Now get to the internet and search for companies in any area of business. You will notice that most of them are hardly ten years old and are international or national brands.

Those trapped in yester years, are missing crucial benefits of the information age. For starters, you can get clients or customers from other jurisdictions without spending a cent because of the internet.

The world is actively moving to the internet. Every continent today has a considerable number of internet users, who cannot be ignored.

Now that we have briefly gone through the stages of human development, it is now possible to place yourself somewhere.

Which time-in-life trap are you in? If you are not anywhere close to the traps, then look ahead, as every change brings them.

Alvin Toffler, the futurist in his book The Third Wave, talks about the fact that each stage of human development is more intense than the previous.

The new age pushes out the old culture and society.

Added to the above, William G Huitt in his speech "Success in the conceptual age," observes that every stage of human development, gets shorter with technology as the key driver.

The hunter-gatherer stage took several thousand years with the knife, spear, bows and arrows as the technology providing success. There was more of human muscle than brain at work.

The agricultural stage took a few thousand years with the hoe, the plough, the tractor and harvester bringing success. Life was faster than during the hunter-gatherer era.

The industrial age took a few hundred years, with the factory at the epicenter, and labour and markets bringing success.

The information age it therefore follows, will take an even shorter time.

Nevertheless, because I am discussing the information age it is critical to note that those with the knowledge and skills required in this era will reap the life style this age brings.

Examples abound today of communities trapped in the ways of yester times. Resources are scarce, but old practices have refused to give way, and a state of conflict with early adapters to new ways is almost unavoidable.

Here is another story to drive the point home.

In our country today, over seventy percent of the population is dependent on agriculture, and mostly subsistence. Here we meet our friend John, a descendant of a family that has depended on agricultural to meet all its financial needs.

The family did not purchase the land, but rather awaited their turn in the family tree queue to inherit what had to customarily be passed down the patrilineal [4] tree.

John's polygamous Grandfather had some five hundred acres of arable land to his name.

Befitting his wealth status, was a homestead complete with three wives and twenty-five children, five of whom were girls. Under normal customary practice, the girls got married off, hence staking no claim to land.

John's father, being amongst the twenty eligible siblings to inherit land equitably, got twenty-five acres for himself.

---

4.   [4] *Patrilineal. Father's side. Matrilineal is the mother's side.*

In line with tradition, John's Father, urged on by John's Grandmother, begot all the relatives that he could. I.e. to have children who are commensurate in number with his known relatives. The children are then named after them.

Traditionally many African communities encouraged the birth of many children as a way to counter the high mortality rates experienced before the advent of modern medicine and improved hygiene practices in Africa. It was hoped that when diseases struck, some children would live on to carry on the family tree.

Losses from natural calamities such as drought, lightning and floods, contributed to the practice. This tradition of bearing many children seems to have outlived the principle, now that mortality rates have plummeted.

John's Father in modern times fathered nine children, two of them daughters.

With the challenges of diminishing wealth within the wider family; on account of loss of economies of scale brought about by subdivisions, John's unmarried sisters get caught up, and now have children of their own. But tradition comes in handy.

Unmarried daughters with children counted on land inheritance to secure the future of the children. Therefore in our case, John and his siblings all inherited just under three acres of land.

Now our good friend John came of age and begot five children. In addition, in his time certain realities set in.

For starters, the weather patterns are no longer predictable; meaning that sufficient food is no longer a guarantee in any one planting season. Secondly, input costs are at their highest in years.

These facts push him to the City, in search of a job to augment his farm's income.

Armed with limited education, and equipped with unmarketable farming skills in town, John settles for a security job guarding a residential property.

Upon earning his first salary, he moves to dwell in a shanty, commensurate with his income. A good friend had hosted him just to settle him in to city life.

For John life begins all over again; he has to cook, wash his cloths and do everything for himself. Life has moved him from a comfortable resident in the village, to a fraught dweller in the city.

Fast forward. The new challenges soon get John thinking, and he realizes that it is not worth staying away from the comfort of his family, in a lonely job where hand-to-mouth is the order of the day. In a frank confrontation with life, John realizes that the hitherto friendly tradition is now his worst enemy, and sticking to it will not help much.

Whereas tradition secured him a piece of land, what he got was not useful and commercially viable in isolation.

He also realizes that after being of the mindset that aided in creating negative competition for land via inheritance back at home, the same mindset propelled him to town to create competition for meager jobs.

"Mindset, regardless of where one is, will always return consistent results that are commensurate to that mind." David Mugun.

Feeling it for his children, who in the first place cannot get a decent education from his modest earnings, let alone the less than an acre they are entitled to, he is convinced that the little city life exposure has served its usefulness, and armed with his twelfth pay cheque he heads back to the village.

As expected, relatives come in all forms and shades, not only to welcome John, but also to receive enlightenment of city life. However, John has other plans for them.

Over the next two years, John brings together the wider family to specialize in different crops, and assures them of a stable market secured through his city contacts.

Seventy percent of the original five hundred acres are now under different crops and everyone is happy, in fact happy enough to have the patience for economically beneficial meetings called by John.

The wider family has come to terms with the reality of what subdivision causes, and John has convinced most of them to accept consolidation of land and instead of inheriting land, swap that practice for shares. The next goal is to modernize the farming techniques and increase production.

John had the choice to either remain as a Night Guard, or get back to farming profitably. I am sure that many people refuse to confront realities, and remain languishing in various stages of the time related traps. Just to recap; **mindset, regardless of where one is, will always return consistent results that are commensurate to that mind.** End of story.

Clara Winston - "Time, for all its smuggling in of new problems, conspicuously cancels others."

"Graduation is only a concept. In real life, every day you graduate. Graduation is a process that goes on until the last day of your life. If you can grasp that, you'll make a difference."
Arie Pencovici

7

CONCEPT OF TIME TRAP

This would have been part of the upbringing trap, but the significance of time to us today has forced me to bring it out separately.

In certain cultures, time is viewed as that which is planned, and is experienced at the intended time. It is for this reason that diaries are put to use. An appointment at 12:00pm has to start as planned.

Other cultures view time differently. They view time as immaterial, until it is experienced.

If a wedding was to take place at 12:00pm, the bride would be better off arriving at the Church, or wedding venue, say thirty minutes earlier.

But this is immaterial until the Grandmother, Auntie or some other relative has received a gift from the would- be in-laws. In this case, time matters after the gift is handed over. It is the physical experience of the gift that gets the culture clock ticking, and the lack of it brings it to a halt.

Therefore, either side of the time concept divide can take advantage of the other, depending on what is at stake. This is a challenge that widely travelled people encounter.

Let me domesticate this trap using real life experiences.

One evening a few years ago, I was in the company of some Bankers. As was expected, their experiences at work came to the fore.

I recall one of them narrating how scared he and his colleagues were on Monday mornings because their boss, who was from the Western world time concept, would not take any excuses for turning up late for early morning seven o'clock meetings.

"If you get a flat tyre, you have to drive on then deal with it later," he moaned. This was on the strength of an employment contract indicating that work officially started at eight o'clock.

Let us face it. In a country where unemployment rates are high, some sacrifices are in order. Or is it debatable?

As the discussions went on, a group of Insurance Executives joined in, and lavishly poured their sympathies on the Bankers because, the insurance company they worked for, had a culture akin to the "African concept of time". One of them mentioned how their idea of an early morning meeting, is one planned for 9:00am but commencing at 9:30am.

Fast forward. Five years later, I met the same group of Executives, and as fate had it, none of them still worked for either the Insurance Company or the Bank. The Insurance Company was now in the hands of owners operating on the western time concept.

What had happened is that in both instances, the western time concept prevailed in tandem with ownership. External investors took control of these companies. This is bound to impact on us significantly, as we globalize at faster rates than before.

Because of this phenomenon, we will have no time for Government Officials who turn up late for scheduled functions. We will also not have time for airlines that take off behind schedule, and then spin-doctor excuses such as "we are taking off late as a result of a loose wire connection detected in the system." End of story.

The concept of time trap, which as we have seen considers that time is immaterial until it is experienced, can have very negative connotations.

Take the case of a corrupt public system, otherwise meant to provide services. Where manual intervention within the operating framework is the order of the day, it becomes very easy to extort service seekers. In Kenya for instance, we had an era of court files "disappearing," and hence justice was not dispensed on time.

The accused would conspire with Court Officers to frustrate cases that were not in their favour. In such a case, time is surely immaterial, unless it is experienced via a judgment.

Time was equally immaterial up until money was realized by the bribing Officer.

Here is a short story that analogises the concept of time trap, when experienced in its harmful form.

While at a business lunch a while ago, my business prospect dashed in late and went on to explain his delay.

His business partner had been involved in a road accident the previous night, and he had been to see him a little earlier. My sympathies were soon heightened by what the accident victim had encountered.

Because, a Good Samaritan rushed him in, the objective was to get him to hospital quickly. He had neither a medical service provider's card, nor his Identity Card with him.

Therefore, the poor man had to stay on the Hospital floor, until there was proof of ability to pay.

Since the man was in no state to communicate, the Hospital Attendant stuck a label on his forehead with the words "unknown male". For sure, time was immaterial regardless of the emergency, until money was experienced. My prospect, and a few of his friends, helped sort the medical bill.

We then settled down to have lunch, albeit with disdain for the Hospital.

"There is a time for everything. Doing the right thing at the wrong time, or the wrong thing at the right time, leaves you wrong still".- Unknown

8

GENDER TRAPS

Men and women are different in a number of ways. Many experts have written books extensively on the subject. I will stick to a few of the differences to make the point on gender traps.

There are things that each gender is better at than the other.

Bear in mind the law of averages in what I will be focusing on. If you ask women and men to choose one of the following two topics to discuss, then your guess is as good as mine.

1. Discussions on car maintenance and racing.
2. Discussions on where to shop for household items.

Let me add a few more.

When watching television, who is more likely to advocate for soaps as opposed to documentaries? What about fiction movies versus those based on true stories? When changing into bedtime gear, who is more likely to leave cloths on the floor? In addition, who is most likely to neatly tidy them away or throw them in the laundry basket?

Men and women have many areas of interest that neither gender can appreciate at the same level. So as you look at the problems that we go through, please ensure that you are not caught up in the gender trap. Getting independent opinions from the opposite sex is critical.

It is story time again, and two short ones will help emphasize the point. I will however add that this topic is the subject of several books, and you are encouraged to read more on the subject as this chapter is not exhaustive.

A number of women led magazines, initially had a lukewarm reception at their infancy by male dominated media houses. A friend recently pointed out to me about 'Living' magazine in America by Martha Stewart, who no doubt is one of the most influential women of our time.

In my friend's own words, "It is today a leading magazine with a wide readership, whether men like it or not". The best media houses of the time she adds, "Could not appreciate the content". The reason is the gender trap. It is like organizing a writing desk the right-handed way, for someone who is left-handed.

The male Editors went through the content of the manuscripts from a man's world perspective, and missed the point. So a big part of the market was forced to see things incongruously. Just imagine how many advertisements targeted at women never reaped maximum potential.

End of first story.

A while back, the company I worked for at the time was involved in an industry wide exhibition. All participating companies were allocated an exhibition stand. For some reason, the men in the event committee enthusiastically got things going.

The stand had to be equipped and prepared appropriately so that the visiting public could be enticed to pass by, and by doing so increase our chances of closing business deals in addition to getting ranked for an overall prize from the event organizers.

All of the men were quite content with the final appearance of the stand, given that we had all the items in our tick list in place.

An hour to the official opening of the event, two ladies in the team walked in to take up their respective duties.

The men were very cross with the ladies and focused on why it took them so long to reach the exhibition area. The ladies seemed mad at us, because in their words "the stand is plain!"

We all rushed for the tick list and asked them to point out what was missing. That list was quickly thrown away and the ladies walked away saying 'we will be back shortly".

True to their word, they were back with ribbons, balloons, buntings, flowers and a pen for the visitors' book.

We all stared at each other wondering how all that was missed out.

End of second story.

We must ensure that we are not finding solutions by taking advantage of traps that support our view of issues. The formulas proposed, if used well, are allies that will take you away from any traps. Men or women haters exploit the gender trap to gain a following.

John Wayne - "Getting rid of a man without hurting his masculinity is a problem. 'Get out' and 'I never want to see you again' might sound like a challenge. If you want to get rid of a man, I suggest saying, 'I love you.... I want to marry you.... I want to have your children.' Sometimes they leave skid marks.

9

ALL TRAPS PUT TOGETHER AS IN REAL LIFE SITUATIONS.

We have covered six life traps. Viz: - Upbringing, Dinosaur, Information, Time–in-life, Concept of time and Gender. These may not be exhaustive, but they nonetheless bring to life entrapments that cause us problems.

The bonus for you is that this book gave you the definition of a life trap at the beginning. This enables you to identify many more traps that have not been covered in this book.

When all the traps afflicting an individual come into play, they provide opportunities or challenges to different people. The importance of these chapters is to allow you to see how to avoid exploitation because of life traps.

As we cover the chapters on exploitation, you will see that **ignorance and untamed emotion are the lubricants that allow the life traps to take negative effects on us.**

Ignorance is the single word encompassing everything you do not know, and is not just limited to the illiterate.

Emotions come in different forms and one can exploit your anger, fears, feelings and passion to your detriment. Take the case of a troubled young woman who seeks advice from an elderly woman, but instead gets hurt when she learns that her elderly friend just took advantage of her situation to get very private and personal details. Instead of a solution, the young woman got arm-twisted into submission and henceforth is at the mercy of the elderly manipulator.

Ever heard the phrase, *"If you cannot convince, confuse"*? If there are ten of you in a room listening to me, and I do not sound convincing to only three of you, I will most probably have confused the other seven and gotten away with 'murder'.

Let us now go chapter by chapter on exploitation.

Napoleon Hill - "No one can make you jealous, angry, vengeful, or greedy — unless you let him."

10

POLITICAL EXPLOITATION

Elective politics is a game of numbers. Numbers come in the form of voters, or money, or both. A competitive game thrives on outwitting your opponent, using whatever means possible. This is where the entire dart about a person be it true or made up, is exposed with the aim of influencing voters the other way.

Politicians exploit life traps to win votes. We know that within a country not everyone at any given time is of the same intellect, knowledge, creed or exposure. Herein lie some of the gaps that fuel politics.

When you have voters with the following attributes, then you have a political farm ready for harvest.

The politician will spot the weaknesses, and find a suitable casing to secure followers.

1. A constituency of people boxed in by strong upbringing traps that are used to fuel emotions, when brought to the fore, threaten the economic opportunities brought about by a differentiator such as race, religion or "outsiders".

2. Unemployment arising from a skills gap with no immediate remedial solutions.

3. Voters ready to bite the dust blown their way by the dinosaur trap that has kept them holding on to the irrelevant past in the wake of new technologies.

4. People ready to fall into the misinformation trap, catalyzed by a politician's ability to exploit the ignorant by sounding like an expert in a field he knows little. *Confidence convinces.*

5. A constituency of voters gullible to gender traps bent on isolating and disadvantaging the opposite sex.

The statements above depict what is replicated in every Presidential or other political office election world over.

It is even worse when a candidate is entrapped in yester years.

Election rigging and violence is the hunter-gatherer mentality brought forward. The use of humble occupations, such as that of a plumber, to reach out to the masses exploits the aspirations of those largely sidelined by several life traps.

In your own country, I am certain that you can spot the traps that politicians used to exploit while campaigning for high office.

In contrast, traps can be put to positive use to lift communities out of trouble. It is easy to know which of your leaders is advocating for the bridging of life traps. Education, training, imparting of useful skills, and provision of opportunities that bring out the best in everyone are equalizers that leaders worth their salt must pursue.

It is story time again. In fact, two stories on political exploitation. I call them the knife stories; firstly because they depict the kind of competition that cuts off political opponents, and secondly because knives play a part in both stories.

Words such as deceit, conspiracy and intrigue; like shadows never leave a politician's life.

Even if he means well, these actions will still manifest, although in varying degrees, just to distinguish one politician from another.

In Kenya, a tropical country, a story is told of Tropicalised Machiavellianism amongst politicians themselves. Fortunately, ugali[5] gives us the perfect analogy.

We eat ugali all the time, given that it is our staple food. Politicians have given it another meaning. There were times when many of them met in seclusion for the famous "ugali eating sessions" in officially restricted areas. (**The newspapers of these particular times confirmed this bit.**) This was when money and other favours were exchanged for loyalty.

These were the days when Politicians were openly paid to defect to other political parties so that the opposition was weakened both inside and outside Parliament.

Almost two decades on Tropicalised Machiavellianism has gone a notch higher.

We have politicians who "fatten" and "kill" you at the same time. Because of their love for "Ugali", we have seen witty political leaders outdo their opponents. Sample this.

---

5.   [5] *Ugali. A meal prepared from the floor of maize, millet, sorghum or dried cassava. It is prepared by mixing the floor with hot water, and cooking it to a tasty finish with the aid of a wooden ladle that ensures a uniform texture is attained.*

Once firmly settled in Government, a Political Party Chief invites all his unsuspecting fellow political leaders to a feast. He personally cooks the "Ugali", for strategic reasons. Some things just cannot be delegated.

The delicacy begins its final journey from the cooking pot onto the serving pan.

It is then shaped into a ready-to-serve cake-like state, for good effect when it is presented at the table.

Just as the "ugali" is moved from the kitchen to the dining table, the host conceals a sharp knife underneath the much awaited food, and marks its exact position for easy retrieval later.

Because of the hunger pangs significantly built up by the host's deliberate slow cooking, the invited guests focus on the food. The "good" host first takes his portion and partially eats it, so that the guests are confident that there is no poison in the food.

And as intended, the knife is under the host's portion of "ugali". Soon everyone is focused on eating. The hungry men must eat to their fill, and functional logic dictates that one must outpace the rest when swallowing the food so that he can eat more and possibly get to his fill. All are thinking very much alike and eating very fast.

With everyone's eyes firmly focused on the "ugali".

The host senses that there is not much time left, and in any case, more "ugali" only makes all the politicians stronger and formidable.

Therefore, he holds the concealed knife firmly in his hand and without warning strikes dead his identified rival to the throne and says "Amen."

His bewildered guests scamper for cover when he declares that he has another prayer.

"Ugali" denotes the resources and power that obviously the politicians want to control, consume or enjoy.

The gesture of eating first before the guests is an act of killing two birds with one stone. The first, is a show of approval and comradeship, and second to safely attach a hook of dirt on the intended targets. The master is supposedly leading by example, albeit unknown to the public.

The knife denotes a knockout card up the sleeve.

The witty politician, strikes when the intended target's concentration is taken away by the tasty meal prepared by him.

For you the common people, if you ever receive a similar invitation from the Chiefs, know that there is no such thing as a free lunch, someone always pays. It could be immediate, or strategically delayed until the time of maximum effect is nigh.

The second story is not tropicalised. It is from the Eskimos who live on ice.

If there is an animal, that closely embodies a politician, it must be the fox. The saying **"as cunning as a fox"**, *summarises what I mean. However, it is the Eskimos handling of the animal that is perplexing.*

Eskimos live amongst foxes, and for their own safety, and perhaps some warm fluffy coat, they must kill them.

They have an ingenious way of killing the fox. They first kill a seal, collect the blood, and then dip a sharp knife in it. They allow the blood to dry on the knife, then repeat the process over and over again, until the knife has several coats of blood, in much the same way that your wall at home has an under coat and a consistent overcoat of paint.

The handle of the knife is then firmly fixed in the ice such that, from the ground upwards it is only the scent of fresh smelling blood that gets into the fox's good nose.

The knife's temperature is obviously below zero degrees, and the fox licks it with a very warm tongue at first.

Then the cold, which as we know is an effective anaesthetic, soon mutes the sensitivity of the fox's tongue.

At this point, the fox cannot tell the difference between what it is purportedly licking off the cold knife, and what is actually oozing out of its numb tongue; repeatedly shredded by incessant licking of the sharp knife.

The fox is unable to tell that it is swallowing its own blood, and soon becomes weak. It first runs out of oxygen, then energy and finally, the inevitable happens. It falls to its death. The Eskimo, besides being safer by one less fox, now takes from the fox what he wants.

The Eskimo simply went for an easy kill in the form of a seal, and without hunting down the fox, managed to kill it.

Now back to our politics. In the scheme of things, who do you think is: -

The poor seal?   It depicts a lesser thing, sacrificed for a bigger political cause.

Who epitomises the knife?   It symbolises something so fatally obvious, yet presented in an acceptable manner.

Who is the fox? One who is usually cunning, but this time almost effortlessly beaten at his own game, and contained successfully leaving the Eskimo with energy to spare for other activities.

The fox was lured to its death using what it likes most.

Who plays the numbing role of the ice? This is usually something, or someone, so close to you but working against you. Usually one that is difficult to suspect.

Finally, who is the Eskimo? This is the chief planner / schemer.

To conclude, let me take you to the Brazilian jungle, not for the samba dance, but for a final analogy on politicians.

There is a species of wildcat whose delicacy is a squirrel-sized monkey known as pied tamarind. In order to kill, the cat lures its victim by mimicking its call.

So all the cat does is spot a potential victim, then hides nearby and calls its victim to the dining table.

A familiar call to safety, ends up as a fatal ambush. Moreover, borrowing from the domestic cat, it effectively hides all the evidence of a kill by licking itself clean, and passes for a meek animal.

Politicians may sometimes work in a way that attracts you to them, only to realize when it is too late that you were taken for a ride.

Do you feel that you are somewhere in the scheme of things when you reflect back on all three stories?

Politicians! No offence meant. It is just about covering the topic on how several politicians exploit fellow politicians and the masses.

"In order to become the master, the politician poses as the servant."
--Charles de Gaulle

11

BUSINESS AND FINANCIAL EXPLOITATION

The Citizens of any country are consumers of products made available by business channels. It is the responsibility of every Government to protect its Citizens from harmful products.

The nature of a businessperson is to continuously look for moneymaking opportunities. Many businesses are useful to the communities that they operate in, and go the extra mile to contribute through corporate social responsibility.

Others do not care one bit about society, but instead focus on the dime they can squeeze out of the poor Citizens.

Businesses dealing in counterfeit products and drugs harm the communities that they serve.

The consumers of these products are often those entrapped in a number of life circumstances that force them to be on the cheap side of life, and do not realize that cheap is expensive.

The businesspersons in these exploitative affairs are of hunter-gatherer mentality, reincarnated in the industrial age. This category includes tax evaders.

Financial exploitation is perhaps the most obvious life trap related abuse. From individuals to Governments, financial exploitation exists. The phrase *"every man has a price"* is true to many vulnerable people. There are many different levels of prostitution targeting either gender in our world today. Every one of them has a mix of attributes and realities, some of them very harsh, which determine the price. The red light district is driven by money.

There are instances where government officials have betrayed the responsibility entrusted on them by the public, and dipped hands in the till. Government and sports officials have been scandalised for gaining financially in exchange for much needed votes when seeking the rights to host big global events.

Idle youth are a target for drug traffickers, and body part traffickers, who get vital body organs for rich clients.

We know that poachers in our Game Parks kill animals for precious tusks, horns, hides and trophies. All these have ready markets.

This chapter can be very long, given that money is the root of many bad things.

Unknown - 'A money-lender serves you in the present tense; lends to you in the conditional mood; keeps you in the subjunctive; and ruins you in the future.'"

Proverb - "Avarus animus nullo satiatur lucro — A greedy mind is satisfied with no amount of gain"

André Maurois - "The greedy search for money or success will almost always lead men into unhappiness. Why? Because that kind of life makes them depend upon things outside themselves."

12

INTELLECTUAL EXPLOITATION

We have very many different disciplines that we depend on for a living. The better we are, when compared with colleagues or peers, the greater the influence that we can exert on issues around our specialisation. Intellectuals can exploit weaknesses in society for their own benefit.

There are cases where scientists and intellectuals have rushed to patent money generating ideas, or inventions, that they have come across from people seeking their advice. Worse still, there are many cases where unique plants and multibillion-dollar generating microbes useful in various industries, have been cloned or synthetically reproduced without the permission of the originating third world country.

There are intellectuals who switch positions, depending on political correctness of the subject at hand, especially if money will be made or lost.

Ignorant communities have played guinea pigs when drugs are on trial, and there are musicians whose copyrights are not respected.

Nicholas Chamfort - "Covetousness is a sort of mental gluttony, not confined to money, but greedy of honour and feeding on selfishness."

Brooks Atkinson - "The evil that men do, lives on the front pages of greedy newspapers, but the good is oft interred apathetically inside

13

RELIGIOUS EXPLOITATION

This is where many have, and continue to fall victim. All the life traps form the backbone for religious exploitation.

Many cults that have predicted the end of the world have exploited weaknesses brought about by life traps to win over their followers.

There is a whole subject on religious exploitation, better told by experts of religion, but some of the links exploited are very clear. The same gaps used by politicians are at play in the methods of the religious raconteur.

I choose to keep this short because we all have examples of this kind of deceptive exploitation.

Marian Anderson - "A singer starts by having his instrument as a gift from God ... When you have been given something in a moment of grace; it is sacrilegious to be greedy."

To conclude the life traps that we have gone through so far, I will share a phenomenon witnessed in the Kenyan banking industry throughout the first decade of the 2000s; and more so, for me it became clearer from 2007 when I joined the banking industry.

This story definitely uncovers several life traps, as observed in a real life situation.

My story has a title that says it as it is. I wrote this article, and kept it safely away from all until now for this book.

THE TIME WHEN PLENTY OF EXPERIENCE DOES NOT CARRY THE DAY.

There are times when it pays to unlearn what we know, and then learn new things all together.

My view and regard for experience has changed lately. We are sometimes engulfed by time traps that make us rely on experiences, that do not support business fundamentals of the day.

One of the biggest financial events ever witnessed in Kenya happened courtesy of a building society turning into a bank.

This building society in fact never grew on its expected core business of buildings. It grew in a sector earlier shunned by the bigger banks, and perhaps this kept it below the radar screen. It targeted the common man and woman shunned by other banks.

Perhaps, if it had huge buildings all over, then this might have aided many to visualize its potential. Those who took notice however, are the non-bankers, who found a new home for their money and business dealings.

Many of the most experienced bankers scoffed, frowned and predicted doom and gloom for the new kid on the block. I had just transited from insurance to banking, and the most experienced bankers seemed to have the ability to see a bubble that the rest of us could not see. Nonetheless, we acted in perfect resonance with our bubble-reading colleagues.

I finally realized that we got the shape right, but misread the object. It was an invisible egg, not a bubble. You see, a bubble bursts to release nothing more than air, period. An invisible egg bursts or breaks open to reveal the life it contains in it, and a young one comes into the world in the form of a new way of thinking, hitherto unknown to the experienced bankers.

As the bubbles predictions became louder, so did the list of accolades that the new bank accumulated. The awards were local, regional and worldwide.

These awards came from bodies that our old bankers had a lot of respect and time for, as they also looked forward to similar recognition.

The predictions then changed in form, and a finger pointing at Government emerged. The Central Bank was now quietly accused of going easy on this bank on the stringent Know Your Customer (KYC) requirements, whilst expecting the rest to tighten the same. Whether this was true or not, is for another day.

The conventional banker could not comprehend the speed with which the customer base of this new bank was growing.

For clarification, KYC requirements amongst other reasons make it harder for ill intending people to open accounts, as it enhances traceability.

Away from the glare of the bubble noise, and unknown to most people, was a monster in the making. The mother of all recessions was forming like a hurricane, right in the back yard from whence the finger pointers and their trainers come from.

Despite all that had been said, nothing has stopped our bank in focus from growing, both within and outside of Kenya.

Let us examine what was happening, and why the bank has not stopped growing.

First, our banking systems were inherited from the British at independence and for a long time, nationals of the old British Empire headed many.

It is no secret that new things get old with time. Old is not always golden. We believed that everything said or came from a first world country was as good as new, and could be relied upon.

Some people in the old first world, became too lenient with financial matters and changed the way the world does business. What ensued was an economic recession that we have all come to experience during our lifetime. That is when I heard for the first time, the term subprime market.

So where is the relationship between the recession, the bubble that never was, and the new bank?

It is now widely accepted, albeit quietly within the Kenyan banking circles, that the dust raised by the creation of a new template by a new comer, triggered what was referred to as the "inevitable bubble" that never was. The old and hitherto all authoritative template, contrasted sharply with the new one.

The new bank left many gasping in its wake, and exposed very unlikely soft under bellies.

As a guide, when more than five percent of the participants in any situation in life embrace a new phenomenon, then know that change is inevitable.

This was the first cue that was ignored, and as a result the bank progressed further, breached the ten percent mark, then twenty percent, and steadily grew its customer base to over fifty percent of all bank accounts in the country.

Secondly, the decision making process in the banking industry came to the fore. Local banks are faster, because the ultimate decision makers are locally based.

The foreign owned banks have their principals residing abroad, besides having predetermined models cast in stone. Some of these models and speed of decision-making when tested against the quicker process available to our bank in focus, meant that the "first-mover advantage" grounds were changing.

New product after another got off the conveyer without much reply.

Thirdly and very surprising, was the fact that a system can have very deep impressions on one, and even way after they are out of the environment, that inculcated in them the thinking process.

A number of leaders leaving multinational banks have carried along with them practices and systems designed to work well only in those banks, and literally **cut and pasted** the same into some locally owned banks that they got a chance to head, or work in.

This happened without regard for size or prevailing culture, just as our staple food, delicious **ugali,** cannot end up as so if prepared in a microwave oven. It just needs the tried and tested simple cooking method that we all know of. This has left some banks worse than they were before. I liken the experience to a body that rejects a transplanted organ.

Fourthly, experience came to the fore. Ironically, some of the most experienced had no transferable experience. A number of people had worked all their lives in established banks, and had no business start up experience, not even at branch set up level.

In this particular case, a senior manager had worked all his life at a well-established multinational bank that at the time of his arrival to the country was closing, rather than opening branches in many parts of the country. Therefore, he had the unique experience of closing branches but none at all at planning to open new ones.

I know of a planning session convened by this manager. Unbelievable is the word for what he did, despite his 26 years of banking experience.

Managers of new and old branches were called to a meeting, and then given the same annual targets on the strength of the managers having similar work experience.

So, similar experience alone he thought would bring the numbers.
These numbers were then committed to the Board of Directors by management. New branches that had not broken-even, were expected to perform at par with the older ones.

So on paper when one was added to one, it equaled two; but in reality the new branches were still at the "trusted brand" building stage and needed more support in that area and not more targets.

Fifthly, and related to the earlier points, is the reality that people tend to do, or build best what they know. Some of the foreign managers adopted systems that favoured support roles over the business functions.
The result was poor morale to the business teams, and the bottom line then remained elusive.

Sixthly, interpretation of ground dynamics, when measured against an imported template, causes a lot of trouble. For example, what is actually a Small and Medium sized Enterprise (SME) business in Kenya, is categorized as micro business because it fits the description of a model bank out of the country.

This may create an attention mismatch at the relationship level.

All these and other pointers, aided in the phenomenal growth of our bank in question.

Square pegs never fit round holes.

We should have taken the cue earlier and discovered that; atmosphere never subscribes to a "cut and paste" approach. We should have taken the cue from two things.

One, we ought to have been proud, and challenged at the same time that we gave to the world a word that is big business. The word "safari" is widely used world over. It is big business in the tour and travel industry. We should be proud that we gave the world an appropriate word to use, but the world out did us in its use.

Secondly, sometimes lessons given to the world come back home in style, just as the UK gave to the world football. The world has taken it back to it as evidenced by the number of foreign players who turn up for premier league teams.

They often play better football compared to the descendants of the inventors of the game.

It is no longer surprising, but both pleasing and psychologically healing, to see that the banking industry in Kenya is now more vibrant thanks to a local bank that helped change the working template of the industry. Today, locals now head some of the big foreign owned banks.

Therefore, not every very experienced person can help you. Ensure that you always take sound advice. I.e. the advice given must logically relate to the fundamentals at play. End of story.

14

HOW ARE CHALLENGES OR PROBLEMS SOLVED?

Problem solving follows one of two main approaches.

It follows either a heuristics approach, or an algorithmic one.

Heuristics, a Greek term means to "find" or "discover". This approach works well when quick solutions are required for immediate application. These include rule of thumb, the trial and error method, taking an educated guess and the use of common sense.

Whereas heuristics do lead us to solutions, they do not work all the time. In most cases, it will require huge budgets to achieve the desired results if applied to bigger projects.

Algorithms are about proven formulas, or sequences to problem solving. A recipe is one algorithm that guides us to cooking a specific meal.

Algorithms work better and faster, and provide desired results because of the defined steps laid out before commencement. Algorithms are way passed the discovery stage. Heuristics can have an element of an adventurous discovery, especially when trial and error is used.

When you hire a Consultant to fix a problem, they follow a series of actions that finally lead them to the solution. The Doctor, the Accountant, the Scientist and even the one who wishes to start a new relationship, all have a formula.

Formulas make us systematic and pragmatic. Without a way of reaching a solution, we just react and might even worsen the situation. Having a formula keeps you in control.

I now move to practical examples in different areas of human life that can use my formulas

I have two formulas or approaches to problem and challenge solving. I will explain all of them as I demonstrate applicability.

1. PReCoRePER
2. NIDER.

PReCoRePER is a seven-step approach that reads out as follows.

1. **Problem** / idea / theory/ challenge
2. Required **Result**
3. **Concepts** and options to finding a solution
4. Determine **Resources** required to finding a solution
5. **Pick** best option(s)
6. **Execute**
7. **Review**

NIDER

This reads:-

1. Where am I **Now?**
2. What is the **Ideal** situation?
3. What do I need to **Do** to reach the ideal situation?
4. **Execute**
5. **Review.**

These seven and five step processes are not prey to the traps we often encounter. They are very much result oriented.

The formulae keep you away from reacting, and perhaps making things worse. They give you the discipline required through the motions of thought that come in an orderly manner to deliver you to your destination.

Finding the discipline to follow these steps may take time; considering that, some of our traps have been with us all our life. Being conscious of this is good enough to give you a good start.

I will use five examples to illustrate the applicability of the first formula in different situations. I suggest that you follow through the example that is in your area of interest. My five examples are:-

1. Math, determine the speed at which a car travels over a given distance.
2. Business – Why sales went down and how to get them back up.
3. Gardening – Choosing suitable houseplants for Ann's house.
4. Health Solution - Finding Tony a solution to his weight problem.
5. Legal – Your neighbour's activities are disturbing the comfort of your little ones. This fifth one is a self-paced exercise, having followed through on any, or all, of the earlier four examples.

Please go to the example of the formula illustration that best suits you.

EXAMPLE NUMBER ONE – SOLVING A MATH PROBLEM.

Let us take a simple mathematical problem and apply all the stages of the first formula.

Let us assume that a car travels a distance of 120 kilometers from point A to B, and takes 50 minutes to reach point B from point A. Let us determine at what speed the car was travelling.

So first, we write the formula.

1. Problem
2. Required Result
3. Concepts and options to finding solution
4. Determine Resources required to finding solution.
5. Pick best option(s).
6. Execute
7. Review

Step one: We know the problem is mathematical and of a car moving from point A to point B.

Step two: The required result, is the speed of the car and is in kilometers per hour (KPH or Km/hr.)

Therefore, it is wise at this point to determine Km/hr.

We have 120 Km and 50 minutes. Therefore, we must convert minutes into hours. An hour has 60 minutes, so we convert using the fraction $50/60 = 0.84$ hours.

Step three: The concept to reaching our result is by way of a formula. We use the formula: - Speed = Distance over time travelled. $(S = D/T)$

Step four: The resources needed to solve this problem may include paper to write on, a pencil, a calculator and eraser to help make corrections.

Step five: Now we need to pick on one option to reach the solution. We have no other option but to use the determined formula in step three.

Step six: We execute now that we have everything. So to get the speed, we write $(S = D/T)$ and get the answer in Kms/hr. So we write $S = 120$ KMs $/ 0.84$ Hours. $= 142.86$ Kms/hr.

Step seven: We review our work against the steps and move on to the next one.

Please note that part of step two you can argue could be handled in step three because the concept of converting minutes into hours is via a formula.

I chose to handle it earlier, to keep the formula simple by working in kilometers per hour to avoid confusion.

If you love math, you can try this seven-step formula to solve different problems.

EXAMPLE NUMBER TWO – SOLVING A BUSINESS PROBLEM

You think that your small business does not warrant an operating system. You recently realized that your sales have plummeted over a given period.

You are the type that is always on top of the game. You have just returned from a motivational seminar for business owners and while you were away, your Manager ran the business.

The Manager recently made purchases of merchandise so that he could run the whole month without having to spend more time with suppliers hence focusing more on Customers.

Your cash count and stocks tally. At first, you think that some of your Customers were scared off while you were away, but a quick survey of your top twenty Customers reveals that all is well, and you move your attention elsewhere.

Another survey, with the medium to small Customers, shows that they have reduced their purchases from your business. Now how do you solve of this problem?

To keep you keen to follow I will give you a hint of where the problem lies. The Manager overstocked the business with what he believed was needed by the big Customers.

The small business owner decides to get a Consultant to unlock the problem. The Consultant quickly gets to work and goes through some steps.

1. Problem
2. Required Result
3. Concepts and options to finding solution
4. Determine Resources required to finding solution.
5. Pick best option(s).
6. Execute
7. Review

Step 1: The problem at hand is to find out why cash flows have gone down over the last one month the business owner was away.

Step 2: The required result is a return to higher cash flows.

Step 3: Concepts and options to reaching a solution are:-

- Use of existing information. In this case, the two surveys on big and small Customers.
- Examination of all the business records over the last one year, including the period the business owner was away.
- Additional interviews and discussions with a wider sample of Customers.
- In-depth discussions with former Customers.
- Employ ratios that show where the business levels were before, and where it is now.
- Use of research tools such as graphs so that the picture of the business is clear.
- A stock taking exercise to determine stock volumes.
- The list can be longer, but let us stop here so that we do not lose sight of the illustration.

Step 4: Based on the concepts above, the required resources are:

- Questionnaires for gathering information from Customers.
- All book keeping records, together with all transaction records.
- Time needed to hold discussions with Customers.
- Adequate knowledge of business research.
- Required stationary and computer to *operationalise* the exercise.

Step 5: Picking of suitable option here means we pick all as they all work in tandem.

Step 6: Execution time now follows the order of preparing questionnaires, scrutinising all the business records to find out where the fluctuations occurred and to pick out all essential points to help us achieve the desired results. Populating the results in the computer and drawing conclusions. With all these, the conclusions will point us in the direction of the problem and an opportunity to recommend remedial action.

Step 7: Reviewing the whole process before getting back to the business owner with the solution.

Therefore, this particular example should clearly give you the confidence that you too can be a business Consultant.

EXAMPLE NUMBER THREE: GARDENING - CHOSING A SUITABLE HOUSEPLANT

Gardening is a favourite practice for many people. Indeed, the majority of families would like to have their own garden, or at least have some houseplants, depending on available space.

I have a passion for houseplants however, without proper attention; plants die or lose their good health and end up looking very bad. Houseplants are as diverse as the conditions they thrive in best. A tropical plant cannot do well in the North Pole.

Every house has it conditions. Even those in one locality may not contain the same plants. A friend who loves houseplants, but does not know how to choose the correct type, motivates this example. She has had plants before and waters them regularly, but they never do well. So how can we help our friend find suitable plants for her lovely home?
First, we get our allies; the seven steps.

1. Problem
2. Required Result
3. Concepts and options to finding solution
4. Determine Resources required in finding solution.
5. Pick best option(s).
6. Execute

7. Review

Step 1: The problem at hand is to find suitable plants for Ann's house.

Step 2: The required result is to have the most suitable plants available for Ann's house.

Step 3: The concepts and options to finding suitable plants are:

- (Observation) Even before you seek an experts advice, carefully record all the conditions in Ann's house; including natural light available all day from every direction, humidity, current resulting from air conditioning or heaters. Plants are living things, just like we are, and need oxygen.
- Get advice from an expert in your area.
- Search the internet for tips.
- The list of options is long. Before you embark on problem solving you may initially feel blank, but this example seems to oversimplify problem solving. So let us use the three options

Step 4: The resources we need to find the solution, based on the options above, are:-

- A medium to record our observations of Ann's house before we seek expert advice. This could be pen and paper or any of the recording inventions within our possession.

- Zero in on the expert most suitable to advice on houseplants.
- Additional information that you have downloaded from the internet.

Step 5: Pick the best option(s) – In this case, all options will help as you use your observations, together with the downloaded information and the expert advice on what are the most suitable houseplants for Ann's house.

Step 6: Execution.

Step 7: Review against all the steps and then help Ann out.
Was this too simple? Yes. Has it led us to the solution? Yes.

EXAMPLE NUMBER FOUR ON HEALTH –AN OVERWHEIGHT FRIEND.

This example depicts what happens to many of us in modern times. We are so busy with our routines that we do not keep track of what is happening around us.

Remember the dinosaur illustration earlier? It became extinct because of resisting change. It could be you.

Our friend Tony is the busy Wall Street type executive who eats, sleeps, talks and plays the Wall Street language.

He hardly does anything else because time of day seems to move too fast, and before he notices the next day has arrived.

Tony woke up one morning and as usual prepared himself for a busy working day. He was shocked to discover that something was different for him that morning.

For the first time, he was unable to tie his shoelaces. His weighing scales immediately confirmed his worst fears, that he had added weight tremendously.

He has a choice of avoiding the problem by buying slip-on shoes, or thinking differently. His self-esteem is at stake, as it may have an impact on other demanding life needs.

So together, how do we help Tony? You and I could probably benefit from this example.

Let us find our formula.

1. Problem
2. Required Result
3. Concepts and options to finding solution
4. Determine Resources required in finding solution.
5. Pick best option(s).
6. Execute
7. Review

Step 1: The problem is that Tony is overweight and cannot bend low enough to tie his shoelaces. We know that procrastination is what allowed him to grow big.

Step 2: The required results are that Tony should lose enough weight to allow adequate flexibility for him to tie his shoelaces. If we stop there, then we are not helping much. So let us raise the bar so that Tony loses enough weight to lead a comfortable life. Signs will include him wearing smaller cloths. (So indicate by how many kilograms or pounds he must lose weight)

Step 3: The concepts and formulae to reaching the solution include:-

- Learning Tony's routine, favourite food and eating frequency.
- Getting Tony's Body Mass Index – BMI to determine level of obesity.

- A persuasive strategy to get Tony's buy - in. Accepting that a problem exists, is always the first step to healing.

Step 4: The resources to take Tony back to health, will include:
- Financial resources.
- Finding an exercise Consultant or physical exercise expert.
- Finding a Doctor and Dietician to provide advice on Tony's condition.
- A program that Tony will follow and can be monitored.

Step 5: The best option to go with, will come from the advice given by the experts you have assembled.

Step 6: Execute the plan and monitor progress.

Step 7: Review progress.

EXAMPLE NUMBER FIVE – A LEGAL ISSUE IN YOUR NEIGHBOURHOOD

Finally I will let you apply the formula on your own, for two reasons.

First, every jurisdiction has different laws and so it is never a one-size fits all approach. Secondly, with the aid of the other examples, it is now easier to solve one problem on your own.

Your neighbour has a construction going on / or the dogs bark too loud and distract your little ones comfort. You live in a good neighbourhood and want your kids to enjoy their home environment. What will you do to reach your solution? Please use the space provided below.

GROUP SOLUTIONS

This book will not be as beneficial if we do not see how the **PReCoRePER** approach can help in solving societal problems, as well as helping out in the work environment.

THE OFFICE

The **PReCoRePER** approach aids organisations to leverage their professionalism in solving challenges. We frequently find ourselves in planning sessions that require us to brainstorm, then finally agree on the way forward.

Every step of the approach can guide brainstorming sessions to positive conclusions. In the office environment, group dynamics come into play.

Everyone has their view and preferred approach to finding solutions.

The time traps, gender traps, cultural traps and personal opinions come into play and block the team from reading from the same script.

Besides, we all have different tendencies. Some are domineering, others are followers, and some are introverted whilst others are the cement between the building bricks and always return the team to a middle ground.

For this to happen effectively, a formula is required so that even as we argue at every stage of our planning process, we have a backbone to keep the bigger picture together.

The formula helps everyone know where to begin, and know when the end is in sight. Please follow the story below as we delve deeper into problem solving in the office.

In the past, I have attended planning sessions that ended up late every night for three days.

Without the benefit of a formula, the sessions went like a river attempting to find its course by meandering along the lowest levels of the terrain.

The dominant, really dominated. The introverts really coiled back. Those attempting to find the middle ground found themselves floating on the endlessly flowing river of the dominant. The irony all along, was that the rules of the sessions were clear.

The rules included:

- *Speak out your mind.*
- *Give everyone a fair chance to contribute.*
- *Stick to the agenda agreed to at the preplanning session.*

The dominant participants did not allow the rules to come into play, but instead seemed to compete on lengthening every issue at hand. At the end, the buy-in was lukewarm because many participants felt pushed away.

The **PReCoRePER** approach lends balance and comfort to the planning process given group dynamics being at play. Everyone gets to be part of the control, and not the controlled. Within a group the intelligent and the shy seldom speak first and as such, the forum may lack the benefit of good ideas. An appropriate approach is desirable.

When planning your office party or other functions, the **PReCoRePER** comes in handy. No doubt, many work related circumstances need a working formula to guide progress.

Let me give you a chance. I want you to think about what you wish to plan in the office. There is still plenty of time to put it all together. Then share it with your colleagues. You will have the highest chance of leading the planning team.

Please use the space provided.

Problem / challenge at hand.

PReCoRePER IN FINDING SOLUTIONS TO COMMUNITY AND SOCIETAL CHALLENGES

I have deliberately made this the last topic on PReCoRePER because society is bigger than the individuals in it are. It carries with it the bad, and the good, in equal measures.

All the reasons so far discussed explaining why problems exist including the yester macho men, the thieves, rapists, the underprivileged, together with the rich and famous, the spiritual, the talented and all the well meaning part of society.

It would be possible to pull out any type of solution or challenge with equal chances, was society held in a pot. Think of society as a balance sheet. It has assets as well as liabilities, and to balance it the shareholders' equity comes in the form of the positive ideas that a few focused people in society have.

The will to lead in one form or the other, is the bridge that makes all the difference.

We can argue that the Government has in place all the mechanisms necessary for peaceful coexistence. It is also true, that the Government is not the solution to everything.

In fact, when J.F. Kennedy, was the President of one of the most prosperous nations, he told his Citizens to ask themselves "what they can do for the country and not what they expect the country to do for them".

So what chances do other Governments have to effectively sort all problems? **Government is not a euphemism for panacea**.

You are categorised as a part of public affairs by the Government. Without delving into the details of modern day law and order mechanisms and practices of governments, I want to focus on the society from a private perspective.

If you are not part of the solution, then you are part of the problem or an addendum to it. There are many ills that afflict society and in particular our neighbourhoods. We can choose to do two things.

We either deal with the issue at hand directly or tactfully, or mobilise others to find lasting solutions. Alternatively, we sit back and criticise what is happening, with no intention of improving the situation.

You do not need to be a community leader to help in finding solutions. You may find yourself contributing the **PReCoRePER** as the way forward and make all the difference.

Societal challenges need direction, organisation and enough followers to attract any meaningful attention. Organised approaches normally give you a sense of high esteem. This is what you need to be part of the solution.

If you want to contribute to society, pick a cause that you can champion and apply **PReCoRePER** albeit reasonably. Remember that you will face challenges influenced by time traps, gender traps, cultural traps and perhaps challenges from Government and political leaders. The difference is clear when you know what you are doing and the result you want to get.

15

THE SECOND APPROACH TO PROBLEM SOLVING

NIDER

This reads:-

1. Where am I **now?**
2. What is the **Ideal** situation?
3. What do I need to **do** to reach the ideal situation?
4. **Execute**
5. **Review.**

This approach also has a very wide application, including aiding us out of time traps. It is very straightforward.

Let us suppose that I am in a time trap arising from technology. I need to have sound command of a certain package for me to qualify for the next job grade.

This package is useful in supervisory positions. I need to go back to a learning centre. What must I do?

Step 1: Where I am now.

- I have a knowledge deficit that I need to fill.
- Without doing so, my Employer will skip me and promote a colleague.
- This will deny me a chance to earn more.

Step 2: The Ideal Situation

- Have the knowledge and certificate for the supervisory package.

Step 3: What I need to do to reach Ideal situation

- Make time to undertake the package at the learning centre.
- Practice to perfection.

Step 4: Execute the plan

Step 5: Review

Think of more challenges that you are currently facing and work it around this approach.

To contrast NIDER with the PReCoRePER, try solving the earlier examples.

16

THE BENEFITS OF AN ORGANISED APPROACH TO PROBLEM SOLVING

The book so far may have sounded comical to you, or may have inspired a high sense of challenge. Whichever way this book has affected you, I feel that it is important to highlight some of the benefits of having an organised approach.

1. NEVER LOSING TRACK OF THE DESIRED RESULTS

The **PReCoRePER** and **NIDER** rank results high up at the beginning just after problem definition. Because of this early search for results at the beginning, the rest of the process progresses on a path leading to the solution at hand.

When you attempt to solve a problem without focusing on the result, then you will not go far.

In today's world, you cannot afford the luxury of losing track of your desired results, given the level of competition and desire to avoid trouble causing traps.

2. DISCIPLINE

At the national scale, Discipline, is the single most important attribute to saving a whole country. The Army thrives on discipline in order to learn and acquire the knowledge and skills necessary to save a country.

In equal measure, discipline is required in the Army when exercising the military skills and knowledge. This determines if a war is to be won or lost.

Those who ensure that there is discipline are the Generals. Generals and not soldiers, win the war.

You are the General when you arrive at solutions in an organised manner. This is visible to all around you. When you have discipline, you attract a following.

Indeed, everyone with a following, has a formula that gets people to admire their way of doing things. You will hardly come across someone you respect so much and is clumsy.

PReCoRePER and **NIDER** when internalised gives, and makes you a disciplined person.

3. TIME SAVING

Time is a non-renewable resource. When spent, it will never recur but results can recur. When faced with a challenge, many times we find ourselves spending a lot of time figuring out where to start. Time is precious and when well used, gives us a chance to do more.

4. HIGH SELF ESTEEM

Self-esteem is a very important thing to have. Many people find themselves caught up in uncomfortable situations. A high level of self-esteem unleashes endless bursts of energy, enabling you to feel good about yourself, and confidently leading a much happier life.

5. RESPECT

You earn yourself respect first before you get it from others. This is what many crave for, but few find.

6. PROFESSIONAL OUTLOOK

A professional outlook is an important ally to have. Professionalism opens doors to prosperity and greater success.

7. ELIMINATE CONFUSION

The label of confusion attracts plenty of negative energy around you. An organised approach will keep you away from it.

8. CONFIDENCE

Confidence inspires admiration, attracts crowds, pre-empts bullies coming after you, opens doors and reduces unnecessary challenges. So why not have it?

17

THE SCIENCE OF CHANGE

Change is the main theme of this book.

It is important to discuss the science of change to augment the contents thus far, as well as provide an additional tool for predicting the likelihood of change taking place.

Over 40 years ago, David Gleicher and Richard Beckhard developed what today is famously referred to as Gleicher's Formula for Change. All the credit of this vital tool goes out to them.

This formula recognises that most times change is a people process. It could be a Government Policy, a corporate decision or even one at community level.

If you are in sales, this formula can help you predict if your proposition to a customer can result in a sale.

The formula is as follows.

$$D \times V \times F > R$$

D = *Dissatisfaction with the way things are now.*
V = *Vision of what is possible (tangible and concrete).*

F = *First steps that can be taken towards achieving the vision.*

R = *Resistance to the change (monetary, psychological, e.t.c).*

The product (multiplication) of D, V and F should outweigh the overall resistance to change in order for change to happen effectively.

How many times have you been in the situation where you're trying to get something done, get a new process or system implemented, get rid of outdated tools, or maybe even something like losing some weight, and then it just ends up falling by the wayside.

One possibility for the failure is that the dissatisfaction for the current situation either is not very strong, or doesn't really exist. This happens a lot in corporate environments where there is a 'company' mandate to get something done, but there is never an explanation for why the status quo is a problem…

in short, there is not a pressing need for the change to occur, and eventually the initiative will either die a quiet death or is escalated with more urgency.

This also comes into play if you're trying to sell a solution to a customer. You know your product is better, you know and can communicate the long-term benefits, and you know and can communicate exactly how they could implement your solution.

However, if it turns out the prospects really does not mind the current situation; you are never going to close the sale. This is exactly what is covered in Spin Selling (a great sales book by Neil Rackham).

V = Vision of what's possible (concrete and tangible)

When you are trying to change, you are changing to something; but unless you can paint an extremely clear picture of a result that everyone can understand and buy into, you will not have support, and more than likely the initiative will fail.

A detailed vision that people can believe is important so that you have everyone affected pulling in the same direction. If everyone is clear on what the outcome is, then all can start actively finding better ways to solve problems to get there.

It is hard to get excited or make tangible progress towards a fuzzy goal.

A goal of 'Make More Money' might be exciting, but it is not specific and because it is not specific, it is not credible. Does it mean make an extra 100 bob per week or 1,000 per week? My commitment level would be different for those two scenarios, and non-existent without some clarity.

Finally, without a compelling vision (detailed or not) you are not giving anyone a reason to take action. You might be in pain and you might know what steps you can take for action, but without having a destination, it will be very easy to get off course and lose your way.

This is like the smart person that hates their job, but they do not really know what they want to do…so they stay in a job they hate because it is not possible to overcome the resistance to changing without a viable vision of where they are going!

F = First steps that can be taken towards achieving the vision

This is where many change initiatives are bogged down. You are dissatisfied with what you have got going on, you are excited about a clear and tangible vision for the future, but you have no idea how to make that vision happen.

Everyone knows someone that would like to lose weight.

The problem most run into is that it is not clear how to make that happen. They see success stories so they know it can be done, but without having a clear idea of how to start (one that they believe will actually work) the whole process is stuck before it gets started.

First steps doesn't mean you have to have an explicit map for the entire effort, but you need to take action that makes sense and moves the effort forward (towards the vision).

R = Resistance to the Change

Resistance really depends on what you're trying to do. At an individual level, the resistance to breaking habits can be extremely difficult exercising; smoking, drinking, eating are primarily driven by habits (with some substance abuse issues in there as well).

At more of an organizational level, there is still individual resistance, but there's also organizational resistance. People will ask…What's in it for me? Maybe a change is good for an organization over all, but if it makes the job harder for the Sales Department it's likely the resistance will be high.

They will need to feel the dissatisfaction and appreciate the vision individually, to overcome that resistance.

18

THE 53 SECRETS TO HOW TO UNDO LIFE'S AIRLOCKS

READ IN CONJUNCTION WITH THE REST OF THE BOOK.

1)   Life abhors a vacuum. If you do not manage life, it will manage you and it will use anything or anyone to manage you. In the absence of a formula to problem solving, anyone else's formula will come into play. You become a candidate open to exploitation.

Without a formula, you are prone to believing everything you read or hear.

Not everything written in the newspapers, or aired over the radio and television or the internet, makes gospel truth.

When you cannot understand what is going on, you end up a newspaper graduate, and at best a graduate from The University of Hard Knocks (Life) graduating cam laude with a Bachelor's degree in "Please exploit me now".

Without a formula, you turn back to practices of yester years such as in the examples on potbellies and the three generations that chopped vegetables from a limited surface.

2)   Whenever you are faced with a problem, step back and ask yourself if it is a simple or complex problem.

A simple problem is one that is straightforward and does not involve emotion, finances, plenty of time, a health condition and plenty of thought.

A complex problem will have either one, or all of the aspects mentioned. Stepping back gives you time to zoom in to perspective in readiness to face the challenge.

3)   Whenever you solve a complex problem or challenge, always document the steps and resources

used and keep them safe and readily accessible to you. This will make it simpler to solve the next time a similar situation arises.

4)   Similar to three (3) above, remember that your memory is fallible and prone to forgetting discussions or agreements reached. So when you go into a meeting, always have a permanent medium to record the important things.

If you carry loose paper with you, it may be lost or misplaced, but a book or your note pad is a lasting solution you can refer to months after the meeting.

5)   Whenever you are expected to resolve an issue between two parties, never take sides, even if your friend is involved. A good judge listens to both sides before passing judgment. If you are too close to the parties involved, you have to ask yourself if it is worth getting involved at the expense of your friendship.

6)   Always benchmark yourself against reality to see if you are headed into a trap. If so, start working on the solution. Never allow procrastination to be your ally. Ask yourself - What is the reality now? Where am I relative to the reality? Where do I want to be? What do I need to do? Then just do it.

7)   Always remember that the significant problems you face now, cannot and will not be solved at the same level of thinking that you were at when you got into them, or created them. You must tower over the problem for you to see it better, and hence solve it.

Always question what your level of thinking was when the problem occurred. (You could have been annoyed, excited, happy, sick or in panic) You could have lacked the required technology or an enabling environment.

With your level sorted, ask yourself what you require to reach a good level to sort the problem.

8)   Avoid falling into obvious problems such as breaking the law. Equally, avoid hanging around known troublemakers or trouble spots. Association can land you in hot soup.

Staying away from trouble gives you time and a clear mind to see the real issues in a much better way.

9)   Life is not a dress rehearsal. The world is not for the faint hearted. Everyone you see alive won their first race against five million of their type (sperm) to make it to become the baby that is now competing with everyone else.

Therefore, everyone is born a champion. Always know that everyone is capable of something, and many times you will compete to emerge victorious.

The reason why situations in life are always tough, is that when everyone is a champion, then any competing interests can never be a walk over.

10) Allow yourself to have access to positive sources of wisdom. Older people, or those that possess more experience, are good resources in aiding you to avoid re-inventing the wheel.

11) Always understand the other person first before responding. This keeps you in control, as you avert confrontation or disdain. It even pays to ask a question to test your understanding of the subject matter before you respond. Ever heard the saying, "never open your mouth before your brain is engaged in gear?"

12) Find time to confront your fears, and the things you are not good at, if they affect you. If they affect your performance or quality of life, you must deal with them. Nobody else is in a better position than you, to correct deeply embedded trepidation.

I went to college with a lady best described as big and very fat. Every time we had trips or functions, she sat either first in the bus or never at all because she was embarrassed of her size. For the next three years she went on a strict diet and exercise regime, and on graduation day she was freely mingling with everyone.

If she did not do it then, then maybe never, because she soon got into a very demanding eight to five job.

13) Always spot and manage or avoid distributors of negative energy. Such people drain away a lot of your energy, thus affecting your ability to solve problems. Avoid lest you emerge void.

14) You are as strong as the networks you build. Always have a diversified list of friends. You cannot cocoon yourself only around people with your kind of thinking and qualifications.

Have a lawyer, policeman, banker and teacher and just about every career or profession. This diversity will come in handy whenever a problem requiring help from anyone of them presents itself.
There are many times when you just need clarification on an issue or idea at hand while in a conversation. Your expert friends come in handy.

15) Always evaluate your list of friends, and weed out those that are not adding value to you, and replace them with new value adding friends.

A table such as the one below can help you with the exercise of dropping or retaining friends. This ensures that you have access to dependable information and advice free.

Always ensure that they have sound credentials and reputations in their respective areas of specialisation.

Manage the process of weeding out carefully, because people react differently to rejection. Do not solve a problem by creating another one for yourself.

FRIEND'S NAME	VALUE YOU GIVE TO HIM/HER	VALUE YOU GET FROM HIM	IS IT POSITIVE OR NEGATIVE VALUE?	DECISION
ABCZ	123	456	ANSWER	XYZ

16) Always practice problem anticipation, then find suggested practical solutions. This ensures that when problems really do happen, you are ahead of your game.

This also aids in keeping you calm in the face of problems. Many people often panic, and hasten the problem instead of solving it, because their minds are not trained to deal with it.

Think about how you can save your relationship before any real problem sets in.

If you have children, play the game "what would you do if xyz happened"? Say if "I saw a stranger at the gate, what must I do?" This helps them to manage the problems they face with a lot of control.

Do you have a disaster recovery strategy in place? Do you have a fire extinguisher at home? Do you have a list of all emergency numbers that you may need?

17) Never ever expose your weaknesses and the things that are very dear to you to people you do not know well enough.

More so, do not be the kind or person that everybody knows everything about. When emotionally devastated, please resist pouring out your problems to the nearest stranger. There are friendly strangers, and strange friends who are of little use in times of difficulty.

Have different advisers and helping hands for different issues.

There was a man who went away on a three-month business course. He asked a "good" friend to keep an eye on his beautiful girlfriend, his thriving business and brand new car while away.

Fast forward. On his return his "good" friend gave back his run down car, a limping business and no girlfriend. He had switched roles with his friend on the girlfriend.

The "good" friend was always a secret admirer and was handed his chance on a silver plate. He was never interested in the business or the car, only the girlfriend.

The decision to make such a person a friend in the first place, must have been reckless.

18) Never ever, confuse hasty decisions for beneficial quick thinking.

Quick thinking rides on your good command of the situation. You need to have the correct information, the right level of knowledge and the experience needed to move with speed.

Even in times of emergency, the Doctor will always give the next of kin the options that exist to take a decision.
These are informed decisions, coming from someone with the correct information, the right level of knowledge and the experience needed to move with speed. Quick thinking needs a sound foundation.

19) Always have a success mentality. Always have an outlook on life that is positively bigger than your present circumstances. Even if you only have three suits that you wear to work weekly, or can hardly make ends meet, always keep your head high so that you never get distracted from reaching the

bigger goals in life. A mind that thinks success, always has the energy levels required to find that success.

20) Think like a leader, and not like a follower. Followers never sort problems, they follow orders and many times play the role of a flag in the wind.

The leader, on the other hand, provides the wind in the form of influence and direction. S/he is always in charge and can organise.

A leadership mentality keeps you collected and in a position to meet and talk to anyone without feeling subservient. If you think like a leader, a posturing fellow will not cow you to *followership*.

21) Always go for the big things that matter in life. In life, you have *biggies* and *smallies*.

The biggies are the few things that have the biggest impact, while the smallies are the many tiny things that have the least impact but take a lot of your time.

The small things make you work hard, while the big things need a smart approach. There is nothing too big to do. Your thinking makes it so. Whenever your mind drags you to the smallies, ask yourself if it is important and worth your while.

22) Always bring closure to matters that have lost relevance. Never be the bag that forever carries irrelevant grudges and revenge missions. *Grudges have an expiry date.* The lessons though, are indelible.

There are always bigger things to work on all the time. Have a way of burning and exhausting the loads of hatred and negative energy in your tank. This way you create a reserve tank ready to accommodate positive things.

I know of a golfer who often makes the ball take the place of his enemy or bad habit. His tee shots are often long and straight, and are normally accompanied by sighs of relief as he forever releases the bad thought. (Please consult your pro before trying this.)

23) Make your enemies work for you indirectly. Since they always see your weaknesses as free weapons to inflict pain, then let this be the reason not to procrastinate on your weaknesses. Your procrastination is your enemy's opportunity to work on you. Its absence, is your chance to progress yourself. Being kept on your toes all the time, keeps you prepared for any eventuality.

So be positive and take time to correct your weaknesses. This way you become stronger and harder to target.

Also, find smart ways to use their strengths if they surely are the best at something. You can be indirect and use a trusted friend to get what you need from your enemy.

If your enemy is the only person with information on an impending policy change that may affect you, it is best to know of it well in advance through a trusted intermediary.

24) Given a choice out of your own free will by life, it is better to avoid making unnecessary enemies, than to make friends who never affect your life positively.

Unnecessary enemies, often abound from those around you who honestly eke out a living through modest means, or those that you perceive as insignificant owing to your higher status, courtesy of your thinking.

Friends who never affect your life positively are those who never or seldom reciprocate your friendship. **Why make someone a priority in your life when you are not a priority in his or hers?**

Never undermine the low ranking employees at work, or in your neighbourhood. The driver, messenger and the cleaner can get to hear things about you and keep you informed accordingly.

The guards at your apartment block get to see and know what happens when you are away at work.

25) Avoid confrontation with your superiors at all times. Learn more about them and know how to manage them.

Never have your boss on your enemy list, even after you find another job. You will be amazed at the reversing of attitude towards you when you continue to engage him/her. If you initially were at loggerheads then, their silent guilt will always work for you.

26) If you have long-term objectives to attain, always remain consistent and focused. No one with a lottery mentality achieves long-term objectives. One hundred percent commitment may not immediately return one hundred percent results, but over time the gap narrows towards the goal.

27) Only be the early bird when it matters, but never ever be the early worm because you will be caught. Avoid making yourself cheap fodder for your competitors. Always get good advice before

engaging in the big things that matter, and then emerge a fortified and formidable opponent.

28) Never work in unnecessary isolation. Brainstorming is a good way to solving problems. This can be at work, at home or with friends.

If thinking on your own is not providing a solution, then it pays to have a group aiding you to find one. Not all problems are best solved by brainstorming. Pick what works for you. An expert can come in handy.

29) Eat healthy. What you eat has an impact on your body and brain. Eating healthy allows you to be better prepared to solve problems. Please find material to read more about this.

30) Take care of your brain as it is the most important part of you that is required to solve every problem. Exercise you brain so that you can benefit from it when you are in problem solving mode.

You should read more about many brain exercises. Luciano Passuello has a list of 120 ways to boost your brainpower. Visit the website www.litemind.com. You can download a book that serves your purpose from the internet, or buy one at the bookshop.

31) Exercise your body to keep fit. When your body is at its optimum, you avoid a number of body related problems. Be sure that the exercise is beneficial so that you do not fool or harm yourself. Do you have an expert in your list of friends?

32) Find enough rest everyday so that you are always fresh enough to be in problem solving mode. Enough said.

33) Appreciate different cultures. This will help you learn how others think outside of your world. It unlocks secrets hitherto unknown to you, that could be beneficial and it always helps you understand yourself better when contrasted against the new culture.

Remember that every culture is sensitive to its religion, politics and beliefs so that you do not walk into a landmine.

34) Whenever possible, travel away from your home environment as this also increases your knowledge besides; making new friends and discoveries that can prove useful.

When travelling away is not possible, then mingling with new groups of people will do.

35) Keep close to your loved ones. Tension always drains much needed energy. Find things you love doing together, both in private and in public, so that you enjoy life whilst being there when solutions are needed from you.

36) Have time for a good laugh as it is good for the body and brain. Within your group of friends, you will have those that are fun to be with. Find comedies, movies and events that allow you to laugh your heart out. A tantrum saps out more energy than a good laugh takes away.

37) Have time to connect with your spiritual nature and get inspiration. People who claim not to believe in God always call out His name when they think that death is near, perhaps because they are experiencing a life-threatening situation. Do not be one of these people. You need time with God so that you enjoy life.

38) Always manage your finances and resources. It is always easier to spend than to save or make money. If you are not good at financial matters, find a good consultant. Go the extra mile to know alternative ways of making money. Hobbies can prove to be a good source of additional income because you will put your energy to good use on something you like. Get someone to determine for

you your net worth, then see what needs improvement.

39) **Money follows order**. *'Order is to money what a night light is to a moth. Its presence, brings to the fore an irresistible urge to merge.' David Mugun – Author of How to Undo Life's Airlocks.*

If you want to attract money for your business proposal, then be orderly in your approach. Financiers want to be sure that their money is not lent out, or given out, to a bottomless pit.

If you are known to be orderly, chances are that you will encounter less resistance when finding money. Money is always in someone's pocket, and the only way to legally get it to yours, is to face that person and present your case in such a way that order is seen and appreciated.

40) Never postpone what needs to be done, because you will have a bigger workload to deal with the next day. It feels fulfilling to get finished with what is at hand.

41) Find a cause that you can either champion or identify with, that helps others find solutions to problems. This could be a charity that helps put a smile on the face of a needy person.

When you give without expecting anything back to a worthy cause, you get a sense of fulfillment.

On the other side of the coin, find something to do around successful people. Your usefulness to them is a far-reaching endorsement that can solve many of your problems, as well as giving you a bigger platform to help others solve their problems.

42) If you are in employment, start planning your retirement early enough. Know what you are going to do, and start working on it without any pressure. If you run a business, get to know when to retire to a less active role and enjoy life. Very many people can advice.

43) Much as you have many friends to provide advice, it is still important to have a mentor or two to guide you through your career or other areas of interest. Mentors are also good at opening doors of opportunity for you.

44) Belong to an association of professionals, or a group championing areas of common interest.

Being a member of a sports club, or other affiliation, not only grows your network, but also gives a sense of permanence to your credibility. Investment clubs also fit here.

Credibility is a useful ingredient to problem solving. Certain internet sites host useful affiliations that could prove useful to you.

45) There is never an ideal time to focus on a challenge. Timing as a matter of strategy may be prudent, but conditions seldom are ideal.

When you think about flying, the beetle's body shape is an aerodynamic impossibility, relative to insects that nature rewarded with ideal shapes to fly.

First, its wings seem too short to enable it take off successfully.
Secondly, its body seems too heavy for an air bound insect, and should plunge to the ground every time it takes off.

Yet, in reality the beetle takes off and can fly over a reasonable distance. It does not wait to be of ideal shape.

46) Failure is the brother of success. Many times, it precedes success. For a successful first step, the baby must fall. Only then will he have the required experience to focus on attempting to walk successfully.

Some famous man once said that "success is moving from failure to failure with no loss of enthusiasm".

Great success is achieved often depending on how one handles his failures. Let it be the hurdle to jump over, rather than the gate that comes between you and your objectives.

47) Permanent or lasting solutions never come from a temporary mind. A temporary mind is that of a person minding about his business through you, albeit temporarily.

Temporary minds have a short-lived reason and mission. The person who is superficially attracted to you, is a fly by night character. S/he wants some good time and that's it. The guy who suddenly befriends you, just because he wants a favour from your office, may just keep you only a little longer after you deliver.

The businessperson who needs to get onto your panel of suppliers will remain a friend on paper, as long as he is in business. Do not invest emotion and useful time in a temporary mind.

48) Whenever you are involved in sorting a problem, be practical to the situation. Never be rigid. If you are helping a kid, then you must go down to his level in order to lift him out of the problem.

If you are dealing with a member of the opposite sex, then adjust accordingly so that gender traps do not come into play.

49) When emotions are at play, problems get complicated and perhaps out of hand. You could be the one who is emotionally charged, or even walk in to a charged situation.

In such a case, ask yourself if it is worth solving things then. If not, always separate the parties to allow for a cooling off period. Emotions can be distractive if not managed.

50) Allow yourself the benefits of conducting a due diligence on the things that you consume. Are you getting value for money? If you are shopping, take time to check the sell by date. Slight attention may betray a counterfeited product, especially if it is a product you consume regularly.

Whenever you get your new cheque book from the bank, be sure to count all the leaves just to ensure none are missing. If you are on a virtual course or long distance learning, are you enrolled in a recognised institution?

51) Always be the kind of person driven by objectives, so that you have a path and a

destination. Problem solvers have goals and a direction that they work towards all the time.

52) Have time to plan your activities and review your objectives.

53) Be alive, alert, ambitious and enthusiastic. Otherwise, what is life for? It is said that a roach that can smell food, even if it cannot reach it, outlives the one that cannot smell any food at all. Just being alive, alert, ambitious and enthusiastic adds more days to your life. There is plenty to live for.

References.

1. *Nathaniel Branden, PHD. The Objectivist Ethics in An Information Age Economy.*
2. *William G. Huitt. Success in the Conceptual Age: Another Paradigm Shift*
3. *Alvin Toffler. The Third Wave.*
4. *The Wolf Trust website.*
5. *Think Big and Gifted Hands. Ben Carson.*
6. *National Geographic*
7. *Neil Rackham. Spin_Selling .*
8. *Richard F. Beckhard. Agent of Change: My Life, My Practice.*
9. *Richard Beckhard, Edgar G. Schein. Organization Development: Strategies and Models,*
10. *Thomas G. G. Cummings, Christopher G. Worley, Christopher G. Worley. Organization Development and Change.*
11. *John R. Schermerhorn, James G. Hunt, Richard N. Osborn. Organizational Behavior .*
12. *Robert Vecchio. Organizational Behavior: Core Concepts*
13. *Stephen P. Robbins .Essentials of Organizational Behavior*
14. *Jim Collins Good to Great: Why Some Companies Make the Leap...and Others Don't*
15. *Edgar H. Schein Organizational Culture and Leadership*
16. *Several quotations duly credited to the respective sources are used throughout the book.*
17. *The stories told to me by several friends who wish to remain anonymous.*

ABOUT THE AUTHOR

David Mugun is a business mentor, manager, speaker and author.

He has helped several Organizations with strategic and operational issues on the back of his experience in both the Banking and Insurance industries, where he held senior positions.

David is a member of the International Mentoring Association-IMA, Professional Coaches Mentors and Advisors -PCMA and Professional Trainers Association of Kenya-PTAK among others.

He lives in Nairobi with his family.

TEL: +254 (0)728 866605

www.ingramcontent.com/pod-product-compliance
Lightning Source LLC
Chambersburg PA
CBHW051506170526
45166CB00001B/412